Finding a Job in 6 Steps

By Miguel Brines

(English corrections by Cat Symonds)

ISBN: 978-1540666291 Reg. B-2828-16

Contents

Introduction	Page 5
What Happens When You Lose Your Job?	Page 6
What If It Is You That Wants a Change?	Page 11
Chapter 1: Waking up to a New Reality	Page 13
Losing Your Job	Page 14
How to Fill Free Time When You Are Unemployed	P20
How Old Are You?	Page 23
Exercise: Looking for the Nautilus	Page 26
You Need a Plan	Page 28
Being Unemployed Doesn't Mean Being Inactive	P 33
Chapter 2: Me, Myself and I	Page 36
Self-Analysis	Page 37
Exercise: A Brief Presentation	Page 43
Illusions Will Get Us Where the Mind Cannot	Page 44
The Target	Page 48
Is Radical Change Possible?	Page 51
Self-Employment as an Option	Page 55

Chapter 3: My CV	Page 57
Looking to the future	Page 58
Nothing is Obvious	Page 62
Keywords	Page 66
A coherent CV for a coherent Life	Page 70
Letter of Motivation	Page 75
Chapter 4: Market Research and Strategy	Page 78
Do Not Let Anxiety Beat You Down!	Page 79
Create Your Own Plan for Getting a Job	Page 83
SWOT Strategy Analysis For Your Job Search	Page 86
Strategy Example	Page 91
Chapter 5: N*etworking* and Contact Management	Page 95
How to Create Your Own Strategy for Contact Management	Page 96
The Key to Networking: Are You Helping Others?	P 102
Guide to Accessing Interesting People	Page 105
How to Use Social Media to Your Advantage	Page 112
Chapter 6: The Interview	Page 119
Interview Preparation	Page 120
Weaknesses	Page 127
How to Prepare for a Job Interview in One Afternoon	P132
Get Your Job Interview off to a Good Start	Page 135
What Does Ego Have with Your Interview?	Page 138
Difficult Questions	Page 142
Typical Interview Mistakes	Page 151
Negotiating Your Salary During the Process	Page 153

Chapter 7: After the Interview   Page 157
    When It's Not You   Page 158
    When It's You: Starting Your New Job   Page 162

Conclusion   Page 164

Acknowledgements   Page 167

The Author   Page 169

Introduction

Dear Reader,

Before entering the mysterious world of the job search, I had better warn you of your rights. You have the right to speak the truth and nothing but the truth, and you have the right to prove your worth during your job search. Please remember: anything you say can and will be used against you. I always start my professional coaching workshops with this strict warning.

I should also warn you of the importance of forgetting all negativity, avoiding self-pity, and fostering an attitude of confidence when finding a job or moving onto a better one. If you find this too difficult, then what you read over the following pages will be of little benefit.

I understand you may have bought this book because inside you there is a need for change. I often have this feeling. I call it the "continuous improvement" feeling. Because scheduled changes are fantastic. And because I like to challenge life to offer me something better. Most of my knowledge of and experience in job searching comes from having lived through several re-locations and having been forced to "find my own way" in life. I hope I can transfer all this knowledge and experience to you through this book.

These days, it is very easy to lose a job. It will probably be even easier in the future. We should therefore be ready for a changing society, with ever-shortening economic cycles. A society where those better able to adapt reap the most benefits during their professional careers.

Job changes will become more commonplace due to both company and employee decisions. It is for this reason that I have decided to share some guidelines with you. I have included advice on what to do when you lose your job, but I have also emphasised the importance of making motivational changes when it is you that has decided to move on.

What Happens When You Lose Your Job?

Normally, we are left feeling that a part of us has been lost, but this is not the case - we are just evolving! Moreover, change is usually for the better, as I will try to demonstrate. I know many people that have become very successful after losing a job, because they had been stuck in a position they did not enjoy, and they had been forced to learn the hard way that they had new unexpected talents. For example, for my friend Josep, who I will speak about more later on in this book, as for many others, losing his job was just the push he needed to change his path and achieve success.

The first thing you need to remember when you lose your job is not to focus on blame. Instead, you should learn from the experience, understand what you did wrong (if anything) and think about how you could face a similar situation if it happened again. Never blame yourself. Take it from someone who has a tendency to punish his own mistakes! In my case, I have learnt with age how to turn a situation around and I have accepted that one cannot change the past. I have also learnt to prioritise the here and now and, above all, focus on the future. The past is what guides us to the future. Accept any reality that presents itself. Life is too short, after all.

What's more, when you lose a job, it could actually be a good opportunity to redesign and restructure your life. Maybe it is destiny: accidentally stumbling across something with potential for positive change when you least expect it. I see reality through my own lens, and I would like you to see your life through yours. It is a chance to start from scratch, and it could be for the best.

Above all, look forwards, never back. Agatha Christie said it best: "I learned (what I suppose I really knew already) that one can never go back, that one should not ever try to go back—that the essence of life is going forward. Life is really a

One Way Street, isn't it?" Therefore, it is time to sit down, reflect on your next step and prepare an effective roadmap to success. Oh, and don't forget to enjoy the ride!

I believe that success is a natural evolution that can be achieved by anyone, at any professional level. Much like the female protagonist from American Beauty (Annette Bening's portrayal was fabulous!), I believe in success based on continuous hard work. What better opportunity to redefine your career than this momentary pause?

If you still have some time left in your current job (one must be professional until the last day, not just for the sake of the company, but for our own dignity, too), then take the time to say goodbye to all your colleagues. Try to resolve any pending issues. It is important to leave a company with your reputation intact, plan for a smooth transmission of duties, and not take on any new projects unless there is time to complete them before you leave.

Some time ago, I read that we are not linked to the companies where we work anymore, but to our network of contacts, and that is there where we should place the most importance when building our professional careers. And I could not agree more. Your current work colleagues could be the "travel companions" of your future career, so it is vital that you get their contact numbers in your diary before you leave.

It can also be an enriching experience. Now that you know you are jumping from the ship, let down your protective walls and thank all the colleagues with whom you have worked. It is important to close all chapters in your life in a positive way – to leave with happy memories.

When they closed the offices where we were working, a colleague of mine went to everyone's desk to say farewell and he told each one of us something positive about our individual personalities, something he valued in each of us. Do not be sucked up by negative energy: understand why it has happened and work on building your contacts. On a personal level, maybe you could become friends with your colleagues now that you will not be working together.

The time between finding out you are being made redundant (or handing in your notice) and actually leaving a company tends to be a bit difficult. Hidden tensions may reveal themselves. Try to avoid these situations and leave with happy memories. Keep hold of those happy memories for as long as you can. At the very least, hold onto them for as long as you are in your current job.

The key in difficult times such as these is to keep calm and be as positive as you can. If necessary, or if you are feeling tense in some situations, go out for a walk. However, do not be negative or allow yourself to be provoked. Stop negative feelings in their tracks. I remember a friend of mine, Raphael, who, when leaving his job, sent out an "email bomb" to everyone, indirectly accusing various people in the company for the situation they were facing and for his dismissal. If you have not been brave enough to speak in an open and constructive manner, to speak honestly in order to further the success of the company, then what is to be gained from speaking up now? It could end up coming back to bite you. Do you want to be remembered for your farewell "email bomb"? For people to speak badly of you when future *headhunters* call for references? Think it through carefully before reacting. It took Raphael a long time to find a new job and I suspect that email had a lot to do with it. It is a small world, after all, and it is not always easy to hide from the consequences of your actions.

Going to work every day under difficult conditions requires a lot of mental effort. It is very difficult; take it from someone who knows. I have lived it and I see it all the time with those whom I help with career changes. I try to calm them down by asking them "Would you be so nervous right now if you knew for sure that you'd find a job within a few months? Would you enjoy the moment instead and see it as an opportunity to learn from changing circumstances? Stressing about finding a job when you know it is just a matter of time is absurd. Because you will find one. Believe me.

The best thing to do when facing a situation like this is to maintain good relations and open lines of communication with your management and with your employers. Prepare an emotive farewell speech thanking your soon to be ex-colleagues and bosses for everything that they've taught you. Keep a cool head and make sure you do not inadvertently do or say something that you will regret later. If possible, a signed recommendation from senior management is always a nice touch. And that is all there is to it. Chapter closed and now it is time to start a new project.

What If It Is You That Wants a Change?

I have a friend, Erik, who has been in the same job now for at least twelve years. His job title has changed at least three times, but he is still in the same position. He spends all his time complaining (often with a reason), not just about money but about lack of recognition, too. He complains about how he is treated, about the lack of material/verbal rewards, the lack of camaraderie, etc. My friend is a good person, but he is not great at plunging into the deep end and taking risks, no matter how much I encourage him to try. I have managed to motivate him to change certain things, but it is still clear that he will never be happy where he is (and I want him to be happy). So I keep motivating him to change. Once I offered to review his CV, and afterwards he asked me to review his LinkedIn, too. We are on the verge of starting a job search, but he needs to feel comfortable about it or it will never work out.

Changing a job when you already have one is even harder than finding a job when unemployed, as it requires you to change gears – to *click into action*. Not only do you have to overcome the insecurity and fear of change that we all face to a certain degree, but you have to do it on your own initiative, too.

As is the case with my friend Erik, the last straw is often something small - a complaint, a grumble, a disappointment, a difficult situation. We all have moments like that. On bad days, we could give up our job in a flash, on better days we go back to our routine (with varying degrees of enthusiasm, depending on the case). Despite knowing that we have gone as far as we can go in a job, that we have reached a glass ceiling in the company, we continue to persevere with our routine. Perhaps it is because *burnout* has quashed our ambitions. Or maybe we have been too patient and failed to plan sufficiently in our professional careers.

People go through stages - some are longer, some are shorter. This can often lead to contradictions with the changing cycles of the business world, as they do not correspond to our own and they leave us feeling redundant. When we reach this point, it is vital to get out as soon as possible, before the *burnout* kicks in. The best way to avoid reaching this point is to have a clearly defined career plan. Then implement it.

Now, let's get down to business!

Chapter 1: Waking up to a New Reality

Losing Your Job

In this chapter, we are going to look at the reality of unemployment. Regardless of whether you have been fired or whether you have resigned, you are facing a fantastic opportunity to redesign your professional career. You are in a privileged position since most people do not have the time or opportunity to re-design, re-evaluate, and reflect on their career choices. You have been given a chance to make whatever changes you need in order to take a measureable leap in your career.

I will not deny that losing your job can often be a traumatic experience, especially if you are a high achiever and believe in continuous self-improvement.

My father was a self-made man, and I see him reflected in myself as a positive role model. He came from a generation of people who suffered through a great deal of hunger after the Spanish Civil War. He came from a poor family and he had to work twice as hard as many others to climb the ladder as he did, and he climbed very high in my opinion. He made great efforts to transmit that culture of effort and hard work to us, so that we could make a better living for ourselves. He came from an agricultural background that put great value on honest, hard work, and this philosophy was nurtured at home. From a young age, my father made me spend my summers working on our house in the country, regardless of how I was doing at school, and when I say young, I mean very young. Despite all the hard work, I could never thank him enough for teaching me the value of hard work. That is why I understand why change can be difficult. I learnt from experience when I lost my own job. It hit me hard. I does not matter how old you are or how much experience you have, we are all human and we all suffer (although, arguably, a little suffering can be good for us).

I especially remember the first time it happened to me. I was working at a factory and they decided to restructure the company. I had a temporary contract for six months. My boss at the time told me that he would fight to the end for me, but in the end, he could not guarantee my position. I still remember his face. I appreciate what he did and I am sure he did indeed fight for me, but who can justify changing someone's contract to a permanent one when the company is being restructured?

It seemed like the end of the road at the time. Suddenly I saw myself with no future. I was going to work every day full of dread and anxiety. For a 25 year old with very little work experience, impatient for success, full of ambition, and in love with his job, it seemed like the end.

I worked hard up to my last day at that job. I really gave it my all. I continued to fight hard for my position until the last day, despite knowing that the end was inevitable. Thankfully, despite taking a hit, I was strong-willed and I refused to give up (that willpower that often leads us to the most exciting places). I started to dedicate my Saturdays to job hunting and I sent over two to three hundred CVs to the biggest companies in the industry (I smile now remembering those pre-email days: the endless photocopying, sticking colour photographs to my CVs with glue sticks, sealing envelopes.). I knew then that the only solution to get me out of my hole was to be self-motivated and smile. No one was going to do it for me.

Eventually, the unions came to an agreement with the company and my days at the company ended, but it was thanks to that experience that I was able to start an even more successful career, and I have been working in my beloved automotive industry for over 16 years now. The factory ended up closing a few years after anyway, so I would have ended up in the same predicament regardless. Life can be like that, and we should try to accept things as they come. I found it hard back then, but these days I would face the situation in a very different way.

It may have taken me three more months to find a new job but much like a sports athlete, I fought hard and gave it my all. I did my best in every single interview I attended. I bought a nice suit with the money I had left from my previous job. I paid for trips to Madrid and Barcelona to attend interviews out of my own pocket (in the 90s most companies did not pay interview trips). When I returned exhausted from these interviews, defeated like a tennis player after a difficult match, I would listen to music - loud and powerful when the interview went well, and quiet and sombre when things did not go to plan. Until one day, I attended a wonderful interview in Rubi (Barcelona) and I was offered my first job in the automotive industry. Then I relaxed.

Finding a job can be exhausting, I know. Especially if you leave your previous company with negative feelings. I understand because I have lived through it. I have lived through the frustration, the pain, that sense of hopelessness, the endless anxiety. Every day I looked at myself in the mirror and said to myself "Cheer up! You can do this!", as Annette Bening character in American Beauty did.

You need to fight to get out of those difficult situations, they just hold you back and stop you from evolving. I managed to eventually, and if I can do it, you can do it too. You have to resist, block out those negative interviews, keep sending out endless CVs Answer difficult interview questions with a big smile and keep it professional. The rest will follow. Never lose your self-esteem when you are unemployed. In the darkest of times, walk with you head held higher than ever.

Sports are my lifeline, especially swimming. I would live in a swimming pool if I could. I always challenge myself there, and it helps my bad back in return. Throughout my life, I have always been able to deal with leaving difficult situations with a mix of positivity and sports. I am also able to apply what sport has taught me about attitude, to my professional life. The importance of camaraderie, for example, striving for continuous improvement, and enjoying what I do.

If you are unemployed at present, or just anxious about life, the best thing you can do is walk. Have a wander, go for a run or go to the gym or swimming pool. It will help you feel a lot better about yourself. A swimming teacher once told me that the secret to any sport is pushing through those "five more minutes" that helps you to grow and improve as an athlete. If you apply these theories to life then you can achieve whatever you put your mind to. If you send three CVs out today and do not receive a response, send out five tomorrow. And if you need motivation just watch any of the videos from the Olympics. The Olympics is full of examples of self-improvement and enjoying what you do.

You can also listen to music. I listen to music a lot. Music accompanies me everywhere because music makes us free; it relaxes me and helps me disconnect. There is a song for every state of mind. The greatest geniuses in life are always an inspiration. Picture some of the greatest singers from the 80s such as Madonna, Bowie or Prince (to name a few). Not only do I admire them for their music, but I also admire them for their careers. Like you and I, they each went through many points in their career where they were not progressing, or they released incredible records that flopped. They all had regular jobs before reaching success but, unlike others, they also had a high dose of self-determination. They believed in themselves and their talents. Yes, as with sports, what matters most is taking part, but a bit of acknowledgment goes a long way.

If you are not a big fan of music, then take your inspiration from art and culture in general. I have the marvellous luck of having a father who was a musician and a mother who is a painter. My advice is to READ. At home we always had books lying around, books on many different topics (not just culture and art). Walk up to a bookcase and pick up a book. Before I made many friends at our summerhouse, I would spend my time reading. It was the perfect combination: the countryside and a good book. Every day I would read a new adventure, get to know a new character, a new story, and let my imagination flow. Reading frees your mind like nothing else, and it feeds you fresh new ideas on how to face life. It is a great way to discover different points of views of the world.

How to Fill Free Time When You Are Unemployed

Now that we have all the time in the world, shall we take some time off, or shall we start looking for a job? Should we go to Bali or should we stay in our hometown?

Some friends of mine decided to take some time-out from many long, complicated and stressful years of work. This can be a good idea; in some cases, it is even medically recommended. Separating from a company is often likened to getting divorced. Many people still have nightmares after leaving a job. It happened to me. I remember recurring dreams about professional situations. I would dream about planning my next day in work, about leading my team and about reviewing reports, and I would often wake up fuzzy and disoriented. In social meetings, I would refer to my former company as "we" or "my company". Luckily, it was just a phase and it passed as soon as I started a new job, which I adapted to very quickly.

In my case, I don't normally allow myself much time in between professional stages. I always think there will be plenty of time in the future to spend my weekends enjoying my hobbies and taking exciting city breaks. I did once spend a few months living in Berlin whilst searching for a job. I still have fond memories of those happy months; long hours spent studying to improve my German and getting used to the *sehr kalt* (very cold) weather. These vital experiences in between jobs can be great learning experiences. Do not dismiss anything and keep connected to your inner self. Sometimes one must accept life as it comes. Live your life and be free. Allow yourself to enjoy those moments of freedom, actively search but whilst enjoying a new experience.

My friend Tere, one of life's great fighters and a real life gold medal winner, spent some time in Bali and Asia after an intense working experience as an expatriate. During that time, not only did she take time to recover, but she also started a new personal phase in her life, which made her a much wiser person. Living abroad can be an uneasy time as it immerses you in a new culture. It can be a period of cultural integration and long working hours, especially if you work in senior management. Many people often need a period of "recovery and decompression" afterwards.

Let's get back to how we deal with things in life and get through the difficult moments. You are facing an indeterminate period of job hunting. You should not just focus on your professional life, but also take time to nurture personal aspects, address those personal challenges or simply do what makes you happy. I remember three years ago someone recommended I start my own blog where I could write about topics that motivated me, and that is where the idea for this book began. It is all about keeping motivated about your passions, pursuing your hobbies and joining new clubs but still staying focused on the job search. The key is maintaining a good balance. I know a few people that have been so distracted by their hobbies that they ended up distancing themselves too much from the recruitment world. Moderation is the key.

When I have tried to help people facing unemployment, I have realised just how easy it can be to lose focus and sight of your goals. Before you know it, there is a two-year gap on your CV. This applies to all professions and positions. Time is never wasted, of course, but the market may have difficulty understanding this period away from work without a convincing explanation. My advice is that if you do not NEED time out; concentrate on developing those hobbies related to your profession instead so that you have something to show for your time on your CV.

I know that planning the future can create anxiety and fear, but keep breathing. The good news is that it is just a phase, a limited period of time. If you follow a good strategy, you should find a good job within a few months. Right now it is time to focus on your hopes and dreams. Nobody can take them away from you.

How Old Are You?

Sometimes, whilst at social events and dinner parties, I hear people say, "I'm having a 30/40/50s crisis". For me, the crisis you have in your 30s is when you realise that the party is over, the one you have in your 40s is when you realise "Oh no, I've spent my life studying and working hard and I've lost touch with what really matters". The crisis in your 50s is when you start to feel the ship sinking and become desperate to recover lost time and enjoy life like when you were young. After every job loss, there is a stage of personal crisis - however we choose to define it.

At times like this, the line between what we are "allowed" to feel and being considered a "complainer" can be a fine one. Obviously, there is no magic solution to this. What I can tell you though is that later on, when you focus on your goal and build a strategy to achieve it, you should stay focused, not lose direction and maintain a clear vision of where you are going and where you are coming from. Life is constantly changing, and it is fine to adjust your objectives, but it is much easier to find the right job if you stay completely focused on a clear goal and stay connected with yourself.

Not to mention that the older we get, the longer it takes to find a job. Obviously, there are always exceptions but, as a general rule of thumb, with age comes diminishing job prospects. One could be disregarded for having "too much experience" or for being deemed "overqualified". Some companies are also reluctant to hire someone over a certain age because, as they claim, with age people develop bad habits at work and become less adaptable to change than younger candidates. Having said that, you should never let age be a factor when searching for a job.

Personally, I believe that jobs are never restricted to age. A good example of this is my friend Agustí who, for many years, was also my boss. At sixty, he is much more mentally active than I am. He plays sports every day and keeps himself mentally stimulated by working hard instead of relaxing and enjoying his pre-retirement at home. Aside from all this, he is also one of the nicest people I know and I admire him very much.

It took some time for Agustí to find a new job after our offices closed, but he managed it, thanks to his incredible perseverance and sense of pride. He even took advantage of his newly found free time to try different professions such as giving lectures. He knew that his perseverance would eventually lead him to a new job, and he was right.

SUMMARY:

I advise you take time to reflect after leaving your job so that you are clear what your next target is going to be. Making a bad decision could lead you down the wrong path. Choose your own journey and keep loyal to your inner self. Moving too fast could stress you out, and moving too slow could make you anxious. Listen to your inner voice at all times.

During this phase, it is important to overcome any negative experiences and not dwell on them for more time than needed. This is what I call the "mourning period".

Exercise: Looking for the Nautilus

Before moving onto the next chapter, let's do an exercise. Dim the lights. Put on some quiet music, the most relaxing you can find. Close your eyes and breathe deeply. Imagine yourself swimming quietly until you reach the deep blue sea and lose sight of land. Slowly dive down, deeper and deeper, until you reach the seabed. In this imaginary dive (with an oxygen tank) you can see the water take on a deeper colour the deeper you dive. There are some plants around you, many different colours, some bright and alluring, others not so much. You make out a shipwreck in the distance. It's far away but you can see that it's big and beautiful. You are amazed at the colourful corals surrounding it. Suddenly, an octopus comes up beside you. It looks like it is pleased to see you. You follow the octopus as it swims in the direction of the shipwreck, interacting with other fish along the way. You reach the ship, have a peek inside, and discover treasure. What a surprise! It is a <u>Phoenician</u> ship, sunk in the Mediterranean Sea during the 1st century BC, and it is full of gold and precious jewels.

Now you are going to start your job search with this same sense of adventure. Notice all the colours of the sea (job market), those that can only truly be appreciated once you dive deep into the ocean. You will need guidance and help from recruiters (octopus and fish), until you reach your shipwreck (future company) and discover the beautiful treasure - your reward for being offered a job at the company. Harness that energy from kicking your diving flippers. Use it to push you in the right direction. Do not forget to savour every moment of the journey, but remember that fish can sometimes be shy. They do not always come to find you; sometimes it is up to you to find them. Even sharks avoid humans, so form a good strategy then go out and find them.

You Need a Plan

The first and most important question to ask yourself is do you have enough financial stability and how long can you survive without an income? Because reality bites, and it bites hard. If you can avoid being bitten, then all the better. I have met many great executives that, out of pride, refused to accept a lower category position and ended up in financial difficulties (desperate to accept any job). I have also seen many people with limited resources, unable to pay the transport needed to get them to interviews. Looking for work comes with certain associated expenses, all be they minimal. We need to prepare for the worst, financially speaking.

You cannot plan a professional career without considering your income. Do not run out of money before finding a new job. Adjust the intensity of your job search to your current and target income.

I remember how painful it was to move back in with my parents in Valencia when I lost my job, but it was part of a bigger plan to use all my finances to travel to Madrid and Barcelona for interviews. During the nineties, it was very rare for a company to pay your travel expenses to attend an interview (it's much more common these days). I am very lucky to have the support of my family. I do not deserve them; they took me in with arms wide open. However, it took a bit of time to get used to after living on my own.

This is a good opportunity to thank my mother for her patience and for constantly adapting to my numerous changes. It cannot have been easy to have a son who was constantly travelling around the world. Someone who changed country/city every 3 to 4 years, chasing bigger and better opportunities. All the people I know that focused on their careers had to change country or city at least once in order to pursue new opportunities. It is not mandatory, of course, but the truth is that the shipwreck could be hiding anywhere in the ocean.

Going back to the topic of financial constraints, the obvious and logical solution would be to find any job as quickly as possible, regardless of level or profile (a position where we would have a competitive advantage and be able to access). Whenever I give this advice to people at my workshops, I can see their face change immediately as I strike a nerve. Life is not black and white though, it is the blend of greys that is our reality. I have seen people bounce from one job to another, desperate to make it to the finish line. However, I have also seen people wait far too long for the perfect job, only to end in a lower level position. It is a lot like finding a partner, really. You can take your time finding the THE RIGHT PARTNER or test the water with many partners and learn how to love through them until THE RIGHT PARTNER comes along. Just like that.

If your financial situation is a big factor, then include an intermediary job in your short-term plan. Think about it calmly and plan for all eventualities. Create a Plan A for now, a Plan B for the short term, and a Plan C for a year from now.

For example:

<u>Plan A</u>: Look for an immediate job in the same sector. This might mean taking a lower qualified position requiring less experience, but it could serve as a stepping-stone to get you to Plan B or C. As my friend, Diana once told me: "Miguel, there's no such thing as being over-qualified for a job. Doing a job well is all about motivation".

<u>Plan B</u>: Look for an intermediary job (skip this phase if you are close to your final target). This is especially advisable if you are making a radical change in your profession (different position in a different sector) or if you are starting a new career from scratch (such as changing from advertising to communications).

<u>Plan C</u>: Look for your dream job.

The rule here is that there are no rules, unless launching yourself into the abyss without a plan which is a bad idea. What is most important, whether you opt for A, B or C, is being aware of your own reality and evaluating all the difficulties that each option might entail.

Although it is important to be realistic, I also encourage you not to abandon your dreams. I have always tried to keep mine alive because I think they are very important, and I would like you to do the same. Go out and search for what you would really like to do, what you do best, and overcome any obstacles that may come your way. One of my all-time favourite quotes is "Hay que pedirle más a la vida" or, in English, "There's more to life than this". Never give up on your dreams. It might take you a while to achieve them, depending on effort and abilities, but if you try hard then you can do it.

I like to challenge myself to improve continuously. Despite having a herniated disc, I once challenged myself to run a half marathon in Antwerp (I was living in Belgium at the time). I had always loved running, but doctors had forbidden it many years before. I made it to the finish line. However, I did not push myself to run any more after that. I had reached my goal and I was able to walk away happy and feel good about myself. Nobody can take away the feeling of satisfaction I got after completing the final gruelling kilometre in the rain, exhausted after battling a steep tunnel. My feet were barely responding (though my mind was strong) but we all cheered and encouraged each other and I made it to the end. That feeling of camaraderie was one of the most magical moments of my life. And I felt so proud of myself. It was just like that feeling you get when you start a new job. Sitting at your desk in your new office, taking on a new management position or introducing yourself as Regional Director at your first conference call.

> ADVICE:
>
> Share your plan with your family and friends, and invite them to give you their point of view. Clarify your reasons: "I want to be... because... so that I can ....". Discuss the pros and cons of your new venture. The support of your family and friends can be vital in realising your dreams. Somewhere between both perspectives lies the path to achieving your goals.
>
> If you are confused and not clear on your path yet, or you know what you want to do but you are not sure where to start or how to put it into words yet, it might be worth seeking professional advice such as a coach or career advisor who can guide you and help you during the decision-making process. At the very least, they can provide you with the information you need in order to make a decision, or even follow up on and support you during your job search.

Being Unemployed Doesn't Mean Being Inactive

It is a well-known fact that the more time you spend out of the market, the harder it becomes to find a new job. Not just because motivation levels drop and positive attitudes begin to decrease (as does self-esteem), but because the feeling of becoming obsolete increases with time. How can anyone fight against that feeling of being left behind? The answer is by performing multiple activities; because activity generates activity, (I have confirmed this with many long-term unemployed people). To use a well-known phrase, it is not about "searching for a job being a job in itself". Instead, we need to believe that "My life now is a job" or "I am my job". We need to convince ourselves that we are working and that our job is working on ourselves. From this mind-set, start performing activities relating to our job search.

Prepare a weekly schedule with strict timetables, such as dedicating six hours a day to searching for jobs. Include some sports activities or hobbies. This is a standard job search schedule. However, I think we need to go one step further and approach the professional market from the inside: we need to interact with the job market. For instance, volunteer for a nonprofit organisation or help a colleague at work for a few hours a week. If you have to work for free then so be it. You are investing in yourself so you have nothing to lose and a great deal to gain. If you change your attitude, it will come across during your interviews.

All this activity can be exhausting. There will be some days when you will probably not want to get out of bed. This applies whether you are unemployed or just unsatisfied in your current job. It's OK. You may think, "I let myself down". I understand because I can be very hard on myself and I expect a lot. However, with time, I have learnt to forgive my small mistakes and moments of laziness. It is OK if you skip a day of your diet, if stop quitting smoking for a day. It is only one day and, provided you wake up the next day twice as determined to succeed (at your job search, diet, or any other personal challenge), you will reach your goal. What matters most is not losing your focus. Keep your eye on the prize and monitor how long you have left to achieve your goal. Always remember that self-discipline is vital and laziness is a can set off a chain of effects. Time is not on your side.

One of the best ways to keep yourself active is by volunteering. You may have read that volunteering automatically increases your personal brand. It is true, but please do not do it purely for *branding* reasons. People may listen to your volunteering stories and you will probably get a certain degree of acknowledgement, but the essence of volunteering is about believing that another world is possible, that things can be different. You have to believe you can make a change and help others. You might decide to volunteer to feel this sense of purpose, but the best reward is seeing how you help others improve their lives for themselves. It is great for self-esteem and personal growth.

I am the kind of person who thinks the world would be a much better place if we all made an effort to pull together and treat each other with mutual respect, independent of race, sexuality, religion or nationality. Can you imagine what it feels like to be a fire fighter volunteering on the Greek coast, saving the lives of refugees? Can you imagine ever being able to feel so proud of yourself?

SUMMARY:

Combining your job search with volunteering is a good option. Being unemployed does not stop you from helping the others. Moreover, feeling proud of yourself is both necessary and beneficial. The same applies to those in difficult professional predicaments, or those longing but afraid to leave their jobs ("burnout").

We should always be proud of ourselves. Find things that help us feel pride.

Chapter 2: Me, Myself and I

Self-Analysis

This is the most important section of the book. What is it all about? It is about YOU.

If you look around, you will see many marvellous, admirable people. They all have one thing in common: they are always THEMSELVES. They are no better than you or I, because there is no such thing as being "better". By being ourselves, we are showing the best of us to the world. If we pretend to be something we are not, people struggle to understand us and to value our unique values.

Believe it or not, one of my biggest role models is Kate Moss. She is around my age if I am not mistaken. Kate Moss interests me because she is a successful professional and she is true to herself (which helped her become an icon). Lately, I have been following one of her quotes: "Never complaint. Never explain", as at my age I am tired of giving explanations about my life. However, the best thing about her is that she is always herself. If you watch videos of her from 1990, 1995 or 2005 (there aren't many - she is not one for giving interviews), you will see her discussing a few topics. You might notice that she is not quite what you had imagined from the photographs. She is much warmer and more welcoming. She always maintains her essence: the innocent girl from Croydon. This is what it means to be true to yourself.

I do not know how to lie. I just cannot do it. I once interrupted an interview because I felt uncomfortable. The interviewer was correcting everything I said and kept asking me the same questions, as if he were pushing for a different answer. I realised that he liked me but he was searching for someone else instead, so he was trying to influence my answers to fit his expectations. I had to interrupt and politely let him know that I did not think I was the person he wanted for the position. In hindsight, the best reaction would have been to complete the interview and then inform them at a later point that I wanted to leave the recruitment process. But another of my favourite quotes is "Never waste time or waste the time of others". On that occasion, I learnt that I could never pretend to be someone I am not. The job just was not for me.

So the first question you need to ask yourself is who am I? On a professional level, am I an executive? A director? A professional from the X sector? What am I like? Why am I unique? Am I assertive? Goal oriented? Creative?

This chapter will allow us to get in touch with our inner essence and learn how to rediscover and sell ourselves. It is not easy (it might even be the hardest part of the process), but it is a vital step.

Let's start with a short interactive game. Write down your profession, as you define it, on a piece of paper. Now, let your imagination wander. It is important to play this game in a quiet place, preferably on a lazy Sunday afternoon accompanied by some quiet and relaxing music. Close your eyes. You are approaching your inner self. What professions is it suggesting? Are there any surprising ones? Add the professions that pop in your head to your list (we are *brainstorming* so it is important to write everything down). You will usually come up with one or two new professions by playing this game, maybe more if you are lucky. Do not limit the list to professional occupations either. I will give you my example:

"I am a businessman, a director, an executive. I have been a manager and I have been an engineer. However, if I close my eyes, I see myself as a childless father, always worrying about others. I like helping people. I see myself as a good salesman, a good negotiator and, overall, a good businessman".

Think back over your entire professional career to find the inspiration you need. The ultimate goal is to define yourself in one paragraph and, if you do it well, assemble the experiences of your personal journey. Order and organise the various pieces of the puzzle and give your career path a sense of direction. Amongst other benefits, this exercise can help you address a common interview question: "Could you introduce yourself, please?" or "What can you tell us about yourself?"

Following the personal method I have developed, you need to analyse the information gathered during the brainstorming exercise and create a detailed and coherent definition of who you are (you will notice I speak about coherence a lot in this book). Use adjectives that define you and your abilities. As we will see in more detail later on, this can often be what helps you stand out from the crowd.

So let's have a play around with some adjectives. Take another piece of paper, preferably of a different colour and shape, and write down all the adjectives you think best describe you professionally. These could include abilities such as being hard working, competitive and ambitious, being a good negotiator, a perfectionist, etc. Try to find words suited to your profile.

Adjectives can help highlight your abilities. If you are finding it hard to define your abilities, try to think about specific work-based situations that you have lived through and remember how you dealt with them. Define the abilities that make you unique so that you can answer the question: "Why should I hire you?".

Once you have analysed your professional experience and abilities (take your time for both), repeat the same exercise for your skills. The difference between skill and competence is learning. However, the difference is subtle and meanings often overlap. Let me explain through an example: you could be a good negotiator because you have a natural competence for it, or you could be good at negotiating because you have studied the techniques, practiced them at work and worked hard to perfect a new skill. Both could even apply: you are a natural born negotiator with perfected skills. Some skills are more dependent on learning, such as having knowledge of quality systems or, to give an even clearer example, Six Sigma Certification, which requires the undertaking of specific training in order to obtain the diploma required for practicing at work.

To end this phase on self-analysis (that is enough self-analysis for one day, don't you think?), let's look at what you want to be. For this part, it is important to have an open mind. Lay down on your bed or somewhere comfortable. Close your eyes and imagine yourself in your dream job. Where do you see yourself? How are you dressed? Smart or casual? What are your colleagues like? What are they doing? What kind of profession do you have? What kind of activities are you carrying out?

You can do this exercise imagining yourself in different places and different situations. See yourself in different potential future professions. Now open your eyes and note it all down in detail.

This exercise of thinking about who you want to be is not easy at all. I remember speaking with a friend of mine, an old boss, Carme: a great professional with a CV that would stop you in your tracks. She was telling me about how she found the ever popular interview question "Where do you see yourself in a few years' time?" difficult to answer. Of course, we all have aspirations in life, but Carme did not aspire to promotion for the sake of it. She enjoyed her work and saw promotion as a natural progression so long as she did her job well. At some point or another, quite naturally, she encountered opportunities for promotion. What mattered most to her was enjoying her work and what she was doing. I know very few people that are involved with their work to the degree that she is. Perhaps it is because what matters to her most is doing a job she enjoys and working for a company that challenges her.

Do not worry if all your aspirations are short term when you complete the following exercise. Think about how important your work environment is to you, what kind of company you would prefer to work at, etc. This section is not only about money and job titles. It is about where you see yourself working, too. Just as important when you are searching for a new job.

Finally, review your professional experience and check for coherence, development and history. Use your notes from the four self-analysis sections: experience, abilities, skills and intentions.

> **EXERCISE: Exercise: A Brief Presentation**
>
> Use this simple template and fill in the gaps.
>
> "I work as a _____. I have been working in the _____ sector for _____ years, and my main duties include _____. I would like to highlight the following abilities: I consider myself to be_____. I was able to apply my competences in my previous position when _____ (the situation). One of my strengths is _____ which I applied in my position of _____ in the _____ sector.
>
> Furthermore, I speak _____ languages at a _____ level which I have continued to practice at _____ . I would like to work as a _____ at _____ (company) in the _____ sector.
>
> Prepare this text and read it in front of the mirror. Repeat it until you can summarise it in two minutes. Do not worry if it sounds a bit forced. I am sure that after you say it out loud a few times, it will start to sound more smooth and natural and you will be able to improvise on the spot.

¡Et *voilà*! We have finished the auto analysis section.

Ready to move on? Repeat after me: "Hey, ho, let's go!".

Illusions Will Get Us Where the Mind Cannot

After our period of self-definition, we are ready to start cruising down the runway as we prepare to take off to our next destination. There are no limits. It is as if we are holding the planet in our hands and we are free to choose any destination.

As humans, we are we can often be pigeonholed at work; we limit ourselves and only relax once we have reached our final goal. The great executives that I have met are two steps ahead, though. Once they have reached a goal, they are already moving onto the next one. It is not about being obsessed with goals and targets, or constantly challenging yourself, but it is about living your dreams. Life is too short to think about whether or not you should be doing something. Just do it! But make a plan before you do. So let's talk about that career plan.

Start from scratch. Ask yourself things like: Where do I want to be in a few years? What jobs will get me there? What do I need to do to get there? How will I get there? Is "there" where I really want to be?

Not so long ago, I spoke to my friend Carles, who I admire greatly, and (as is so often the case when I see him) I walked away amazed at his determination and, most of all, how he has planned his career. He told me that he had opted for an international job, not just because he saw an opportunity to do great things with his future boss, but also because the company encouraged people to develop their own careers on the side. This made it much easier for him to reach a senior executive position if he played your cards right, maximised his performance, and worked hard. You cannot stop someone like Carles. He is always thinking five years ahead and he sees life through his own lens. In life, we have to choose which door to open to get where we want to get. Keep focused on your final destination.

We can learn a lot from Carles's approach. Ask yourself what sort of intermediary job would help you take the next step towards where you want to end up. This is my favourite part of the whole process. It is where we design a strategy, a "three step" process to help you realise your dreams. In order to reach the summit, you must bridge the gap between your dream job and your current job with an intermediary one. Keep in mind that consolidating a position takes minimum 18 months.

ADVICE:

Attitude makes the world of a difference. It is pointless having a dream if you do not believe in it. Starting from today, act like the person you want to be. If you want to be a director, why not start acting like one already?

Unfortunately, society is constantly bombarding us with negative messages, such as "you are too old to get a job", "there aren't any jobs for you", or "you have been unemployed for too long". Clearly, there is some truth reflected in these phrases, but all they really serve to do is create insecurity within us, as we are automatically at a mental disadvantage if we believe the opinions to be true.

These competitive disadvantages can turn into long-term "personal truths". A good attitude can help us avoid these disadvantages and stop us from boycotting ourselves. Let your attitude be your shield.

Not only do I believe in the power of the individuals when it comes to achieving our goals, but I also believe that nothing is impossible. I really believe this and I apply this attitude to everything in life. Do not limit yourself; life is hard enough as it is. Do not stand in your own way before you have even had a chance to begin your search.

Finally, looking for a job can be a difficult and exhausting process, so you have to concentrate and focus your efforts on maintaining a positive attitude. Do not let anyone or anything get you down.

The Target

You might wonder how it is possible to have reached this stage of the process without defining your goals yet. Perhaps your experiences from your last job are preventing you from seeing things clearly, from knowing which direction to take. Whatever the reason, you need to focus on defining your goals, since it is never a good idea to enter the job market without a strategy in place.

We need to stop feeling limited by our last position or the duties we performed. Disconnecting from former jobs is vital. If you do not break the cycle and fight against the current then the job market will keep pushing you into similar positions. Be strict with yourself and vow to never take on 100% of the same duties in another position or take on a similar job.

There are three stages of change:

- Continuity: same sector, same position

- Laterality: change of sector with same position or change of position with same sector

- Radical reorientation: Change of sector and change of position

The bigger the change, the harder the search, but this does not make it impossible.

Evaluate the different options and remember that not everybody is able to change so easily. After carrying out this analysis, some people opt for continuity, others decide to try out a different position or sector, and others are open to new opportunities.

You need to think about what you are going to do over the next few years, decide what your career plan is. We are going to do some work on defining your position and sector now. Think about all those tasks you do well. Those that you are comfortable with and those that best demonstrate your abilities. Skills and abilities are important. Go over your strengths and weaknesses again. If you are not sure about where to start, you can always check your LinkedIn and see how your contacts have evaluated your abilities, or even compare your LinkedIn profile with similar ones.

Later on, we will discuss strategies and methods for implementing them in our searches, but first we need to evaluate the field that you are moving into and what resources and limitations you have. As I mentioned earlier, finances and family obligations can be a big obstacle when job hunting. Languages and availability for relocation can also be a big restriction. Personal circumstances are just as important (or more so) as self-analysis. We live in accordance with our environments, so it is logical that it would have an influence on our decisions. Would you move abroad if you had just met an interesting potential new partner, for example? Would you risk accepting a high responsibility position in another country if it meant relocating two teenage children and removing them from their social environment? These are difficult questions to answer, but they can have a big impact on your search.

I do not want you to take the previous paragraph in a negative way. Sometimes risk is completely necessary for success. For example: I could never thank my mother enough for adapting to the challenges that she faced when she accepted my father challenge and she requested a job transfer from Barcelona to Valencia in order to give us a brighter and better future. It was a difficult change, not least because it meant starting from scratch in a new job and a new city. It was difficult for me, too. I was 15 years old and, for reasons out of my control, I was forced to change schools three times in three years. But, in the end, everything turned out for the best. I live in Barcelona now, which I love, but my heart will always belong to Valencia (where I visit very often), where most of my friends are, and I will never forget my time there. Experiences such as this are vital in life. If you deal with them well, with a positive attitude and an open mind, then they can help you grow. One must always be open to change.

Is Radical Change Possible?

Every time I speak about radical change at my workshops people start to frown, as if they are disappointed or they think I am crazy. Everything looks like a huge mountain. It is obvious that a radical change is much harder than finding a job in a similar position, but it is not impossible.

Radical changes are usually motivated by personal issues or through saturation from working in the same position for too long. Laterally minded people tend to evolve by themselves, they do not need to make any radical changes. For the rest of us, it has to come from inside: it has to be a need or a calling.

To better explain the difference between lateral and radical changes, I would like to introduce my friend Amparo. She's the sister I never had. Not just because I get so much from every conversation I have with her, but because we survived the nightlife of Valencia in the 90s together, those formative soul searching years (sometimes I think a piece of my heart still belongs there, reminding me where I came from and where I am going). Amparo and me, We do not have to see each other often to keep that connection. There are few people in this world quite like Amparito (as we call her in my family). She has incredibly lateral abilities. Not only is she brilliant at everything she does, but she also has a restless urge to learn. She has spent years developing her various skills, training, and working with kindred spirits. She started working on international projects and ended up working in innovation and supporting start-ups. Her career has followed a natural progression, avoiding any confrontation with management. Lateral changes, as I describe them in this book, are changes to your professional life. Small changes, of sector and position, but maintaining coherence with our CVs. Amparito has laterally developed her career over the years (as I like to say, "Learn by doing").

I have seen a few examples of radical change in my time. My friend Josep is a perfect example. It is not that he was unhappy in his former job, but we see him doing so well now that we can really appreciate the positive change in him. Josep followed his own manual for change by listening to what was inside him. He took some time off to disconnect, then began analysing himself. He dedicated some time to understanding what his passions were and how he could combine those passions with his skills and competences as expected (you cannot make a big change unless you really get to know yourself). Not everybody wants or is able to do it. For some, a change of sector or profession is a dream come true. For others, it is like stepping out into the abyss, since there is always an element of risk, which not everyone is willing to assume.

It is not just about deciding where to go next. It is about learning what you want through trial and error. I really admire that trait in Josep. He opened a door and did not succeed, so he searched for another and found his current job, which he loves very much. Josep always says that, in his experience, life is all about adapting to constant change. In addition, I would like to add that if we must learn to live with change, then why not be the one to initiate it.

His first job was not a mistake or a waste of time. It was necessary to help him find his own path. Because there is only one way to do things, and that is your way.

Sometimes one needs to prepare for a new profession and the radical changes it will bring. Disconnecting from the professional world for a year or more (to study for a Master's degree, for example) can often be a good idea. If you need to obtain a degree for your new career then I strongly advise you continue at your current job and plan for your change, studying in your free time.

I still clearly remember the day one of my colleagues from work, Diana, told me that she had received a call for her dream job in Switzerland. It seemed like the opportunity of a lifetime: a Head Office position at a multinational firm, where she would be responsible for an entire department and a large global team. She was so nervous about it. We prepared her CV together and she went to Switzerland convinced that it was "her big chance". When she came back, she did not seem very pleased. She told me that the interview had gone well; they had treated her with respect, evaluated her competences, and challenged her to provide real life examples. She had attended three interviews with various directors in total. The interviews had been long, as is common at her professional level, and when candidates come from abroad, they tend to try to fit all interview into one day, so it had been a long day. Despite everything, though, it had gone well. But (and there's always a but) when she was getting back on the plane she could not stop thinking about being responsible for relocating her entire family to Switzerland, without even knowing if she'd even succeed. Her family had a big influence on her decision. Life can be like that. Sometimes it gives us opportunities that could take us in one direction or another, and we have to make a choice. She chose to stay where she was in the end. Do not worry about her, though. She is happy in her current job, and, eventually, she will find her dream job. I always joke with her that eventually she will have to face the truth and realise that she is destined to become a Senior Director and she cannot hide from her fate. I'm sure that, when she's alone, she occasionally thinks about what her life in Switzerland leading such a big team might have been like.

Self-Employment as an Option

My friend Marian is self-employed: she works for herself. Although quite uncommon in her sector, she decided she wanted to become self-employed as part of a lateral step towards radical change. She decided that in order to expand her abilities and get to know other sectors and positions, she would have to give self-employment a try. She came from the advertising world and now she had ventured into the world of communications, a similar sector but in a different role. I really admire her because she is consistent. She fights every day to be better at what she does, and she has an amazing ability to create stability during periods of occupational instability.

She is happy but she was also happy when she was working for a company with a permanent contract. She is good at adaptation. It is all about owning every situation and recognising that they are all as important as each other. The biggest lesson to take from her story is that she maintained coherence in her career, and self-employment has allowed Marian to access many more companies and collaborate on many different projects, as she gets closer to her goal. In the current changing world, there is a clear trend towards self-employment, seasonal work and having multiple jobs throughout our professional careers. Do not discard self-employment as an option. Go over everything we covered earlier about goals and life paths for achieving them.

> **SUMMARY**
>
> Define your goal and design a career plan. If necessary, choose an intermediary job as a stepping-stone towards your target. Study up on all your options: defining what you want to do, testing new positions and sectors, and following your dreams.
>
> Nevertheless, do not discard the notion that when you finally do reach your goal, you may decide it is not what you actually wanted, after all.

Chapter 3: My CV

Looking to the Future

I will tell you something that you may not have read before. Your CV is your future, not your past. It should include your plans, your dreams, your sectorial targets, and your ideal position. It needs to express what the *next great achievement* in your career will be. Reading through your experience on your CV should give some clues as to your future.

Another important point: every CV you draft is a different version of who you are, a specific presentation for a specific position. Every position you apply for will require a different version.

It is important for employers to explain the type of company you would be working for, as well as provide context for the position and the expectations of the role. On the flipside, it is important for job seekers to listen carefully to what is being offered. Explanations are crucial. A CV must be adapted in line with the job description that led you to apply for the position, and express your experience accordingly. It should be a combination of your former job and the results of your self-analysis. This makes it much easier to gage if you would be able to adapt to the position in terms of skills, competences and experience.

You should also try to read between the lines and understand what the *job description* would represent within the company. A simple example - imagine the following advert:

"Multinational with 4 factories in Western Europe, Headquarters in Barcelona, in a context of global expansion, seeks change oriented entrepreneur with expertise in the field of..."

If you read the job description carefully, you will understand that "context of global expansion" means that the candidate must be able to manage the associated growth, something which can often be challenging and which usually requires frequent site visits, not to mention the political and linguistic abilities required for the position. A position like this could overwhelm someone who is quiet and conservative, but it could also highly motivate an entrepreneur looking for a challenge to further his or her career.

Therefore, it is not just about motivating ourselves and creating a "mental movie" of where we want to be. We also need to read between the lines and reflect what we see in our CV. Be confident that you have the experience, knowledge and expertise required for the position.

You may think, "Given how hard it is to prepare a CV, why should I waste time drafting two or three?" The answer is that we should not apply for jobs that do not really interest us, sending out the first CV we locate in the "attic" of our PC folders. When speaking with candidates and requesting CVS, I constantly hear the phrase, "I need to locate my most recent CV". That is the wrong answer. You should be saying, "I will send you an updated CV adapted to the requirements of the position, this evening at the latest" (if the position really interests us, we should be sending it ASAP). To conclude, we should tailor our CV to each company and position, in line with requirements.

Preparing a CV is one of the hardest parts of the job search process. I can testify to this and I must confess: I never seem to get around to updating mine until I am contacted by a headhunter. I prefer it that way, though, because I am much better at introducing myself over the phone than on paper. Lately, I have discovered that if you are able to explain your CV in a few short minutes, focusing on your skills and abilities, then you will be able to convince an interviewer that you are the right person for the job.

I advise you to write your CV straight after completing the self-knowledge exercise in chapter 2. It will flow much easier once you are in the right frame of mind and inspired, and it is much easier to start a new CV from scratch than modify a previous one.

The standard layout of a CV is as follows: Presentation and Picture (if applicable), Education, Courses, Languages,

Professional Experience, Additional Professional Experience (training, teaching, projects etc.) and Personal Information. Nevertheless, the layout of your CV can always be adapted to the priorities of the position, if justified.

You should always transmit a positive image through your CV, since any negativity might knock us out of the race. I once helped someone review their CV and he mentioned that one of his professional achievements was reducing company losses. I remember telling him that, although I did not doubt it was a great achievement since I had seen similar cases in other companies, I thought that he needed to turn it around and express it in a positive way. So, in this case, substitute words such as "losses" and "negative" with phrases such as "I increased company results by 10%. Then, during the interview, one can expand on the details. It is much easier to explain things properly in person.

Nothing Is Obvious

The people that are going to read your CV do not usually know you, so you must take this into consideration. The biggest mistake we usually make, and I include myself in this, is to assume that the reader is like us; a member of our family; an old colleague. Someone from our circle of friends. We think that with a few pieces of information they will be able to get a feel for who we are. But it is not that simple. Only *headhunters* can get to know you to this degree, and only after taking the time to speak to you and study your CV and profile. We should therefore include examples for everything we say and, if necessary, expand on our descriptions with adjectives.

I am sure there are some things that you would rather keep off your CV. Now is not the time to be modest, though. Every time I read a CV in a small font, with unassuming descriptions, I see shyness and fear of exposure. And it is this fear of exposure that stops people from showing themselves to others. Therefore, and I am sorry to say this, you must be an extrovert in your CV, no matter what it takes. You must open up to the others and give numerous details and examples, especially those that are UNIQUE TO YOU.

You expose yourself the most when you speak about your *hobbies*. That is the most interesting part of a CV! For instance, if you like Japanese culture, what is wrong with saying so, in a positive light? I have to be clear on this: in a positive way. Do not scare people off. In this example, the fact that you like Japanese culture or that you have attended lithographic workshops, in Europe might mean that you're a detailed and sociable person, with a slightly eccentric/creative air. If you practice golf, it can reflect a strategic, sociable mind. Hobby to profession is just a small step. Remember this.

You must be very careful with what you say and, above all, with how you say it (always be positive). Never be afraid to be yourself. On the contrary, be afraid of hiding yourself away too much, of being someone other than yourself, not being you. At work, the more executive a position is, the more that personality is appreciated, as well as individual *management* styles.

Another important point is NEVER lie on your CV. Don't pretend to have done something that you have not. It is so easy to spot. We ask so many questions in an interview, it can be very easy for a candidate to slip up and unravel a lie, and we will tend to discard the candidate when this happens. I personally have encountered two cases of this in my professional life, and they ended up admitting to the lie before being asked about it. You should have seen my Poker face when they told me. For me, as with the rest of the interviewers that I know, lying is the biggest mistake you can make in an interview.

Having a CV that stands out can be a huge advantage. I am going to tell you about my friend Manu. Aside from having an exceptional personality, Manu has followed a very lateral career, in line with her personality and in coherence with the passing the years. She started out as an IT professional, and then became an IT teacher. More recently, whilst maintaining her job, she has studied fashion, creating her own collections. Then she discovered a link between her skills in IT (specifically, social media), teaching and fashion/trends; she became a *Community Manager.* She is constantly evolving as a person, and she managed to find a way to transfer her interests and abilities into a coherent CV, clearly demonstrating her career path.

Mixed profiles are very popular these days (my brother's CV is another example of this as is a balance of IT and audio. More on this later). Do not be afraid of experimenting, but do be careful. Do not lose your essence, your unique personality. Add a professional slant to everything you have done.

Here are some CV "Do's and Don'ts":

CV Do's....	CV Don'ts...
Keep it simple and readable	Include too much text or long descriptions
Keep it to a maximum of one to two pages	Include mistakes or use languages not understood by the reader
Allude to your career aspirations	Mix skills with competences
Base it on the future not the past	Repeat yourself
Show your personality	Write a bland CV with no personality
Reinforce your strengths	Overload it with information. Stick to the key points.
Be precise: don't leave the reader with questions	Leave any gaps in your timeline (you must have been doing something)
Adapt it to the position you are applying for	Send it out before reviewing it
Include personal achievements	Include too many personal achievements.
Keep to the facts and don't bend the truth	Include lies
Make sure it can be skim read	Exaggerate your professional experience

Keywords

I was once recruiting for a position that directly reported to me. It was a key position for me, as I needed a right hand man for managing suppliers. I started writing the job description and realised that it was a much more technical role than I had initially imaged. I did not think it would be too difficult to find the right person though, as the profile already existed on the market. Big mistake. The *headhunter* searching for suitable candidates started sending me people who were not a good fit. Some had had long and interesting careers, but they were not what I was looking for. It is true that I am a very demanding person, but it was required for the position. In the end, I proactively informed the headhunter that I wanted to see CVs with certain keywords only, to save time. I told her to disregard any CVs that did not include those words. Although she was very professional, it took months to find the right candidate. Someone whom, aside from responding correctly to all technical questions, was also motivated and had the right attitude. I hasten to say that those few keywords were a great help in finding the right candidate.

It is therefore important to be aware of the keywords for your sector and position. The easiest way to do this is by looking at the market for similar positions and job offers. Conduct an honest study and compare to see if the required experience matches yours (keywords are helpful here, too). And if you do not have the right experience, do not apply. It wouldn't take long for a good interviewer to detect your lack of experience. I once interviewed a candidate who was very well prepared for the interview from a technical point of view, and he was able to answer all of my questions, providing examples to back everything up. However, he did not have the experience I was looking for, so I had to be honest with him. I thanked him politely for his time and complimented him on his attitude, but I could not continue with the interview.

As mentioned before, I get very upset when someone lies to me. I never lie. Some people accept it better than others do, but for me it is an important issue. If, during an interview, I detect something strange and it turns out to be a lie, it bothers me and, if I am honest, I probably subconsciously discard them as a candidate on the spot (I might finish the interview in a polite way but it will be a shorter one, of course). Moreover, I never forget a name. It is quite common amongst interviewers. So please do not lie. Remember: "It is what it is, so tell it like it is". Being transparent will also help you have more confidence in yourself as a candidate.

Once you have finished writing your CV, you will need to review it and make all the finishing touches. We, the interviewers, can often read between the lines of a CV. We can analyse the data and detect any abnormalities (although we are only human and we make mistakes from time to time). Therefore, the clearer your CV is (self-knowledge) and the more sincere you are during the interview, the better your chances are. You should transmit a sense of "I am who I am, and I am not trying to come across as a model employee". I once interviewed a candidate who was so neutral in his explanations and hid so much of his personality that I could not read his profile. I gave him a second chance and interviewed him again to see what he was really like. It turned out that he had been shy because he was so motivated to give a perfect interview and get the job. In the end I did not hire him as he did not have the right skills, but I am glad I had the chance to meet him and get to know him a bit better than I had in that initial interview. And who know, maybe things will change in the future. The lesson to take here is that nobody wants a cold, seemingly "perfect" robot for a candidate.

SUMMARY:

Do not be afraid to be yourself. Be consistent and clearly explain who you are. Try to find the right keywords for explaining your abilities and use them in your CV, too.

Adapt your CV for every application, but never lie. As we say in Spain, "You can catch a liar faster than you can a man on crutches" (you cannot hide from the truth).

A Coherent CV for a Coherent Life

I remember Alexander asking me for help with his job search. I especially recall when we worked on his CV. Alexander is a great sales executive who, in my opinion, has yet to fulfil his full potential, he has a long way to go still. At the time, I noticed that he was having a bit of trouble articulating his CV (common with most people, by the way). It can often be hard because people such as Alexander move fast in their careers (a good thing) and they are always thinking about the future. There are some points in life when it is important to stop and take stock before moving forwards. So that is what I did with Alexander. We discovered some incredibly unique abilities. Abilities that came so naturally to him that he had not stopped to consider including them. He is a good example of someone that is consistent in his career. He is clear about where he wants to be, but he could do with some time to reflect and self-analyse, to transmit that coherence through his CV. To understand what he wants, articulate it and internalise it.

The ultimate goal is to walk our own path in the journey of life. Only by understanding where we have come from can we find coherence with where we are going. In Alexander's case, this was a very fruitful exercise.

My brother, Javi, is another good example of the importance of having coherence between your life and your CV. Just when I thought I'd seen it all in terms of CVs, one day my brother sent me his, which broke all the rules. This was it:

How did I not realise before that it was possible to summarise and represent your CV through images? Give it a comical slant and maintain coherence? This is an incredible CV (my brother has done many incredible things in his life, this I love). It grabs your attention and really sells itself (although this style would not be welcomed in all sectors).

I always use my brother's CV as an example in my workshops, especially if they are focused on job hunting. Javi printed out 300 copies of his CV on high quality paper, front and back, and folded them in such a way that they could be read like a leaflet, all the important information on display. The keywords were on the front page. Afterwards, he went door to door and had delivered them to all the audio companies in

Barcelona (I did not advise him to do this, he taught himself). It was this coherence that helped him find a job with relative ease. Not only that, but thanks to his initiative, he was soon promoted to manager, and he has a long way to go yet.

The best part of all this is that my brother was loyal to himself. When a CV is written from the heart, it sells itself. Also, his example serves to demonstrate that the design of a CV can always be changed if the sector and company are likely to be receptive to that sort of thing. There is a huge difference between creating a CV for a creative position in a technological start-up and creating one for a finance department at a multinational. Judge each case on its merits. Javi knew that his market would receive it well, so he played his cards, took a risk, and won.

Finally, be aware that the more personalised your CV is, the more you reduce your niche in the market, but you also reduce your competition. In fact, there are many people who carve out their own niche in the market by leading with their personality - CVs sell themselves!

I once went to a conference hosted by a former IKEA CEO, Anders Dahlvig. It was one of the most interesting speeches I have ever attended in my life. The speaker spent an hour presenting his vision and strategy for the company, using just one slide! Not only that, he also had that magical ability, that so few people possess, to be close and direct, speaking to his audience and returning to his slides for prompts and, above all, guiding the talk in a clear direction. It was fascinating! Think of it like this. The slide is your CV and the presentation is your *elevator pitch*. The coherence you present will be the key, but your CV must also be clear and visual so that the interviewer is able to take prompts from it from time to time, just as the speaker did in that speech at ESADE.

Letter Of Motivation

I do not like the term "Cover Letter" or "Letter of Presentation". I prefer to use the term "Letter of Motivation", because this is your first point of contact with your potential future employer (or the person screening CVs). You do not need to repeat what you say in your CV, but some of the phrases you use should match the specific expectations of the position, as well as including a few motivational phrases.

The difference between two candidates with identical education and experience is motivation. I will never tire of saying this. Not so long ago, I saw a job description for a position that I really wanted. I asked the company for the opportunity to send a letter of motivation. They called me (after carefully reviewing my LinkedIn profile, I am sure), and we talked, and then they gave me the go-ahead to send them letter. I spent at least two hours preparing that letter, reviewing my CV, and defining my specific reasons for applying for that particular position. The recruiter from the company called me immediately after receiving it and we met. In person, he told me that the letter caught his attention much more than my CV had.

The letter of motivation went something like this:

> Dear X:
>
> As discussed by phone, I would like to submit my Letter of Motivation for the position of X at your company.
>
> I am a professional from the automotive sector with over X years' experience in the areas of .... I speak five languages at a professional level. I have launched multiple global projects, in locations including Turkey and South Africa.
>
> I would like to highlight that I have professional experience in........., which I thoroughly enjoyed. We instigated the creation of a .... process and, in general, a robust system of .... During my time at the company, we also implemented .... indicators, together with .... process improvements. I worked with a great team of X people and I left leaving a positive mark on the company.
>
> I feel comfortable working in structured international environments and with taking on new responsibilities such as creating new procedures and improving processes. If you take a look at my LinkedIn profile, you will see that my greatest competence, as validated by my contacts, is striving for continuous improvement: my philosophy in life. Furthermore, I have great initiative and leadership skills, which have helped me successfully manage large international teams.

> *I would like to express my sincere motivation to work at your company and kindly ask you to consider my candidacy. I would love the opportunity to work in a creative role such as this, and build on the experience I obtained at …….*
>
> *Finally, I would be pleased to provide any further information about my profile in person in an interview.*
>
> *Yours Sincerely,*
>
>
>
> *Miguel Brines*

The key is, therefore, to show that you are motivated. You have to really want the position, feel that desire, the adrenaline pumping through your blood to have that job. If you do not feel motivated, then you should not apply for the job.

Chapter 4: Market Research and Strategy

Do Not Let Anxiety Beat You Down!

Sometimes, we can be so anxious to contact the employment market as soon as possible, that we do not allow ourselves enough time to plan a good strategy. It might be causing you to miss opportunities with companies that could potentially be of interest.

When is it the right time to develop a good strategy for your job search? In my opinion, it is when you are about to finish your CV. The CV is the milestone that separates two very important phases: the introspective self-analysis phase and the phase where you open yourself up to the world.

The first part of your strategy must consist of benchmarking yourself against your competitors. Before opening yourself up to the world, you must acknowledge and value your competitors. I advise you to have a look at a few other candidates on LinkedIn, find out what you can about their educations, skills and competences. I also advise you to view LinkedIn's top 10 profiles for the position that you want. Compare their skills with yours so you can fully appreciate the competition that you will face and what the market is offering.

Ultimately, it is the market that decides, so analyse it and determine what gaps there might be. These gaps are not always easy to qualify for, but you still have time to take action. Broaden your skills through training. If you struggle with interviews, take some time to train and develop your skills. For example, if you think you have weak leadership skills, implement a strategy in your current workplace to reinforce and develop your abilities. Not only will this help you to improve your position in your current company, but you will also be gaining experience and gathering examples from your daily life for future interviews. Do NOT TELL an interviewer that you can be a good leader. BE one now.

To complete this stage, I advise you to read a few magazines, newsletters, financial reports and forums from your sector. Once you have done all this, ask yourself - Is my CV good enough or should I modify it so it is better adapted to the market?

The second part of the strategy requires conducting market research (first your competitors, then your target sector). Market research is a practical way to approach your target. So if, for example, you were applying for a Sales Director position in the *retail* sector, you'd need to conduct research in this order: retail sector, target companies (their growth, place in the market, future strategic plans, etc.), then research the position itself. It is all about understanding which companies are leading the sector, which are expanding, which are the highest rated, and what their growth values and strategies are. You will then need to analyse if all of this matches up to your expectations. Scouting for work requires a lot of work. You need to find out where these companies are based, where their production centres and R&D departments are, where their Head Office is located, etc. Then, finally, you need to classify all this information by giving priority to those companies you would be most likely to approach. Establish what the best communication channels are for contacting companies: offers, spontaneous candidacy, etc. Think about using your *networking* abilities to get your foot in the door.

    Ask yourself what the best channels for contacting companies in general are. LinkedIn? Recruitment Companies? Headhunters? Which companies can you approach or contact directly? Which companies are within your network range? Communication channels are very important and you must avoid making mistakes. Do your research and adjust your strategy accordingly. Adjust your strategy in line with what you learn about the market. Respond to any correspondence straight away. Perhaps they are not recruiting, they are in the process of re-organising the company, or they are just not able to take on any new staff at present. Find out where you stand and do not waste time. We live in a world of short financial cycles, and this is often reflected at a corporate level.

Summarising, the steps for creating your strategy:

1.- Benchmarking competitors

2.- Market research

3.- Categorising data

4.- Choosing communication channels

The final step involves incorporating social media into your strategy. I could fill a whole book on social media tips. I will keep it brief, though, and limit what I say to telling you that there are two important decisions to make. The first is deciding whether to join in, and the second, if you choose to go for it, is deciding which platforms to use, and to what degree of involvement. The decisions you make here could greatly alter your strategy, and they all carry consequences. Will you be an observer or take an active role? Share content or just read it? Being active in social media requires investing a lot of your time, but it can also increase your exposure and make you more visible to recruiters and companies. In fact, the question you should be asking is: "Can I afford not to be on social media?"

Create Your Own Plan for Getting a Job

You must be realistic about how you approach your sectors and companies, since any mistakes could result in you wasting your time and exhausting your efforts. You cannot go to a gala dinner in your sportswear, and you cannot go to an afternoon cocktail reception in a ball gown or tuxedo. As humans, we respond to what we experience, whether it is proximity, arrogance, etc. I once attended an interview in Paris where the interviewer kept looking at me strangely. At the time, I did not know how to interpret his reaction, Later on, though, I found out what the company was actually like and what values it upheld, and I realised that they were so far removed from the profile and values, transmitted during my interview, that it was no surprise that they had looked at me like I was from outer space. I just came from different corporate culture. Now I am glad I did not end up working there, I would not have enjoyed it. So whenever you are not offered a position, remember that it just was not for you.

When conducting your market research, include an analysis of the company that you are applying to, including as much precise information as possible (what are their values and mission?). For example, if you are targeting automotive companies, there is a cluster of them in Detroit, but there are also many in Europe (Germany, France, etc.). Do you want to work in production or design? In an office or in manufacturing/operations? There will be certain limitations for some of these, most of which will be geographical, so open your map app on your mobile to see just how far you are from your targets and how much of a limitation it could be.

Complete your market analysis by researching the company in as much detail as possible. These days, all the information you need can be found online. Do a search of the top companies in the sector. Limit your research to those companies you would actually want to work at. Create a table including the following fields and use it to rate the companies: turnover, level of product innovation, position in the market, plans for expansion, working environment, management style, opportunities and open job positions. These are all good indicators of the health of the company, but there are many others. Some of this information might only be available through those already working at the company, so if you know of any contacts there, now is a good time to make contact (more tips for managing contacts in chapter 5).

Now is also a good time to compare the information you compiled on your target companies with official lists of Best Companies to Work For. Corporate culture is important. Whilst what matters most is how you relate to management and to the board of directors, we must not forget that we will be spending a lot of time with our colleagues and their attitude and temperament is sure to have an effect.

Categorising all this information in a clear visual way can be useful at this point, using a diagram such as the following:

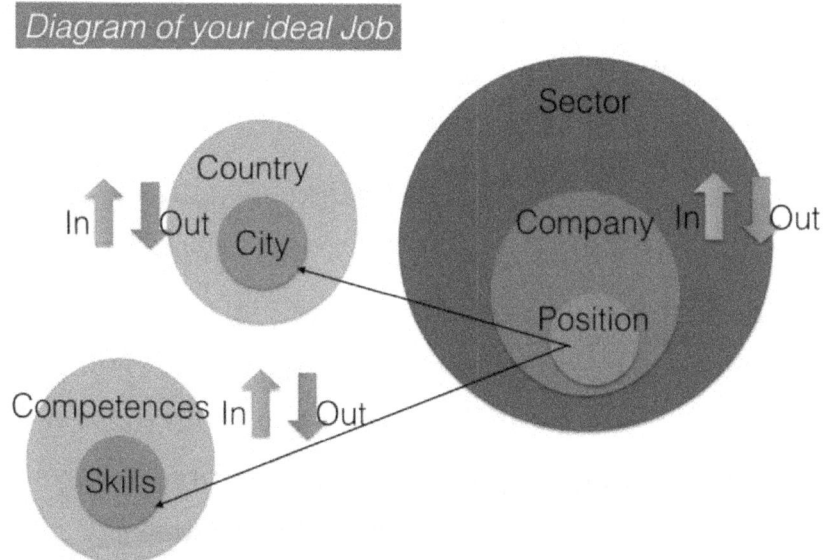

SWOT Strategy Analysis For Your Job Search

If you are not familiar with SWOT, it's an abbreviation that stands for Strengths, Weaknesses, Opportunities and Threats, It's a methodology that can be used when taking on new projects and activities, commonly used in Marketing purposes, but applicable to any field.

In the case of job hunting, the SWOT analysis should be carried out prior to initial contact with the market, not just because it provides an in-depth analysis of it, but also because it enables you to prepare what is needed prior to attending an interview. The idea is to gather information in order to create a strategy for approaching the job market. Before preparing your SWOT analysis, you should have completed your CV and market research, and have a clear idea of your goals. And, of course, you should also have completed the previously mentioned self-analysis phase.

A SWOT analysis allows you to answer certain questions about yourself as a candidate, like "What am I lacking for the position? What are my strengths? What could I bring to the company? Why should they hire me and not someone else? It also allows you to think about the position, company and sector. What do I know about these companies? How do they treat their employees? Do we share the same values? Do I need to improve in any way? You need to classify your answers according to the following:

- <u>Strengths</u>: i.e. One can feel strong in terms of years of experience, or by having an extrovert personality perfectly suited to sales. Our strengths are what make us special and unique.

- <u>Weaknesses</u>: Areas for improvement. Objectively speaking, an example of a weakness could be a lack of knowledge of a certain industry, if we are moving into a new sector. Another example could be lack of proficiency in a foreign language if it is required for the position. Weaknesses need to be addressed with action plans.

- <u>Opportunities</u>: Areas where success is likely. Opportunities could include the possibility of a promotion within a company, or the opportunity to learn new software (SAP, etc.). Another type of opportunity could be accessing a multinational environmental. Opportunities should always be expressed in a positive and optimistic manner.

- <u>Threats</u>: Anything that could be considered an obstacle to success. Do not focus on conflict with colleagues (this could be a problem but we will not know yet at this stage), but instead think of other more tangible threats. A threat could be the risk of being typecast in a particular sector or position if we opt for continuity. Or a target company that is too aggressive about short-term targets so there is a greater risk of failure if we do not achieve our targets.

The SWOT analysis requires a high dose of honesty on your part, and you must be realistic. Whenever possible, the analysis should be based on data, not opinions. For example, to find out if ten years' experience within a sector is strength or not, find out how many years of experience are usually requested in similar job descriptions.

The worst outcome of the SWOT analysis would be a combination of being weak in field together with their being a threat relating to the position. A clear example is working face to face with international clients and not having a high enough level of English. The SWOT analysis must be carried out in full detail so that you have time to address any urgent weaknesses. Do not wait for the interview; react now!

The main benefit of a SWOT analysis is that it enables you to transform your weaknesses into strengths. ultimately; the end goal is to switch your focus from weaknesses to improving your strengths and opportunities.

After the SWOT analysis, create an action plan to improve the abilities required for the position. Address your weaknesses then promote your strengths when you are interviewed.

Swot Analysis in Job Seach

Internal \ External	Threats →	Opportunities
Weaknesses ↓	Surviving Strategy ↓ Reinforce weaknesses	Redesign Strategy
Strengths	Defense Strategy	Offensive Strategy ↓ Active search Strategy

> **SUMMARY:**
>
> The SWOT analysis (Strengths, Weaknesses, Opportunities and Threats) is really a powerful tool for obtaining self-knowledge prior to a job search. It gives us the opportunity to react to a weakness and self-improve before contacting the market.

Strategy Example

Whilst gathering information about your target companies, note down all names and contact information that you find so that you can contact the companies later on. We must not forget that 70% of jobs are filled by contacts: it is all about who you know. I will explain this further in the next chapter.

Some years ago, I went to a very interesting conference with high-level speakers from the automotive world. I like to attend these conferences because you learn a lot from them and they can be a great opportunity to connect with new people. People tell me that I am a good *networker*, and it's true (I think), and I believe it's because I possess two innate abilities: I like meeting new people and I care about the contacts I make over the years, I care about them as I do about my friends. If you sit down next to me on one of my frequent flights and I see you doing something interesting on your computer, or you are reading something that grabs my attention, it is likely that I will start speaking to you and, after landing; you will be leaving with my card. Have you ever walked down to the drinks area on a transatlantic flight? You can find some very interesting people there who, like you, are looking for pleasant conversation. You will not always make a new contact, but sometimes you might meet someone and learn something new about your sector, or find out about professions that you did not know existed. You might even pick up some good recommendations for the country you are about to visit from someone know knows it well.

Getting back to my conference.... that day I listened to talks from four really interesting directors. I saw their management level, their functional strategies, etc. I was particularly taken by one speaker: the comments he made in his speech, the way he approached the sector. I thought that he could be a good boss for me, but at that time, I was already satisfied with my job. After some time, when I started a new job hunting process, I immediately thought about this executive. He was difficult to get hold of. I should have stayed at the conference that day and say hello, exchanged cards and ask him if we could connect through LinkedIn; but I did not. But the law of second chances can also be applied to contacts. So I started moving around and located a contact at the ESADE business school (with whom I had developed my professional career) who had a cousin working at the same company as this executive. I spoke with the cousin and she explained the structure of the company. I got his email through another contact, but I thought it might be too aggressive to approach him directly by email (it is perceived as being even more aggressive these days). So, instead, I decided I would send him a connection request through LinkedIn. I would wait a week to see if he accepted it then, as a last resort, I would write a short email to his corporate email address to reinforce my LinkedIn request. And that is how he came to accept me as a contact on LinkedIn, a great success given that he has a very small network of contacts on LinkedIn. He never replied to my subsequent email though, requesting 5 minutes of his time to introduce myself. So end of the strategy. Game over.

I like to give this example in my workshops because it is a strategy that I defined myself and succeeded with, but the contact was not open to networking. In the end, whether or not someone is open to listening to us is his or her choice. I gave this example for another two reasons. One is to illustrate that we can always reach our contact one way or another, via multiple channels. The only thing that we must take into consideration is whether our time and efforts will be compensated and if the contact will provide added value (it is also important to learn to know when to give up). The other reason is to explain that I did not establish all the information I needed to fully understand the company. I realised later through other candidates that this company had a very "inbred" corporate culture which was very difficult to penetrate as an outsider, since most recruitment was undertaken internally in support of internal career development. If I had known that then (nobody's perfect), then I could have dedicated more time to preparing strategies for other companies instead. But we live and learn from every experience, and every mistake makes us stronger and wiser.

Chapter 5: Networking and Contact Management

How to Create Your Own Strategy for Contact Management

They say that Andy Warhol, New York's infamous master of ceremonies during the early eighties, was extremely shy. In spite of being timid, he was the perfect host at his events at Studio 54, the legendary Manhattan nightclub. I give this example to illustrate that we all have the potential to socialise well and succeed at networking and public relations.

Creating and building on your network of contacts it is something that we should all be doing regularly throughout our lives. The more people we meet, the more we grow to care about them and want to help them, which can only end up helping us in the long term, too. It can also make things much easier when we are unemployed or looking to change jobs. Not so long ago, a headhunter told me that 70% of jobs are filled by network contacts. As people, we work on the basis of trust and friendship.

A contact is, by definition, someone from our circle of connections whom we have access to and with whom we can maintain a conversation. Basically, it is everybody that we meet.

There are varying degrees of acquaintance, from those who we have simply met, to those whom we know better, and friends and family. When it comes to searching for a job, they can all be our allies.

Take a look at the following diagram:

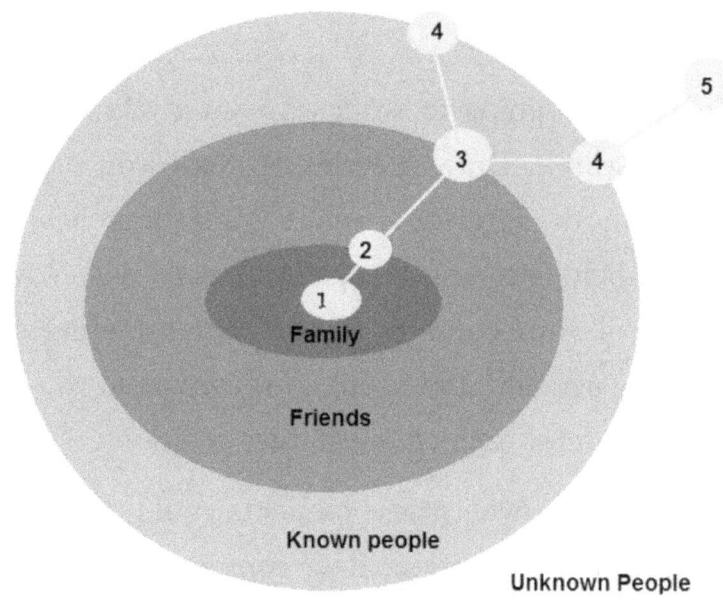

Our contacts can be classified by level depending on how close a contact they are: Level 1 is family and close friends, Level 2 includes other friends, and Level 3 is acquaintances and people we have met. And then there are those that we have not met yet but whom, through mutual association, we are able to contact. In fact, according to *the six degrees of separation*

theory, we can contact anyone in the world though a chain of associations, beginning with people that we know, within a maximum of five steps.

> **EXERCISE**
>
> Now we are going to work on your circle of contacts for your job search. Draw a series of circles on a piece of paper, copying the previous image. Add branches if, for example, you belong to any groups or associations. Now, one by one, add all your contacts to the corresponding sphere (friends-family-acquaintances, etc.). I recommend you draw a different diagram for each of your target positions.
>
> Now consider what these contacts could contribute to your job search (information, new contacts). What do you have in common? What do you both enjoy doing? Are you getting any ideas on how to manage your contacts? If so, add them to your action plan for finding a job.

It is not about rationalising everything and being cold to get what you want. We all have feelings, after all. My friend David holds a high position at a multinational company, but he always finds time to talk with me. He is a natural networker and an extremely professional person. For him, the key to networking is having a sincere interest in people. Sincerity is crucial. If you call someone, you need to be happy to hear from them. If you meet up with people, then it has to be because you like each other, you care about them and you are open to helping them. Otherwise it just will not work. People will get bored if they see that you are only motivated by professional interest.

David also believes that certain sectors, and certain positions, depend on networking. Especially when it comes to high-level executive positions. People live off their networking. Not only in terms of professional movements and promotions, but when it comes to day-to-day contacts, too. In order to be successful, they must benchmark best practices in excellence and mutual support (respecting market rules and ethics) regularly attend also sectorial conferences, and maintain active relationships with their contacts at all times.

So, rule number one is we should only do something if we sincerely enjoy it.

Let's return to the diagram, now. Consider every name and think about how you could contact them and what you would say (if specific).Start creating a plan of action, such as "Lunch with Amparo on Wednesday", "Skype with Antonio on Thursday", etc. Try to organise your weekly activities in line with your social life.

Don't just think in terms of business, it's about leisure, too. Think about everyone on your list and what you get from your relationship with them. What do you want to know about them, and how could you help them out? Because <u>helping others</u> is what it is all about. Understanding what people are going through and appreciating them. Rushing through the process is an option, but it is short-term thinking. People will suss you out and stay away from you (unless they want something from you too). You need to build long-term relationships (today for you tomorrow for me) and, most of all all, enjoy the time you spend with friends and family.

It is not about calling people and asking them directly for a job, but getting to know them as people and helping them out in whatever way you can. If you are looking for a job, mention it in your conversations, but do not dedicate more than a few minutes to talking about it. Conversation should be focused, instead, on natural and informal topics.

Networking can be an adventure. It provides something valuable: the opportunity to meet new people! It is about being open to the world. Let me give you an example. Last time I was unemployed I spent my free time attending events. One day, I went to a presentation for the Hays Salary Guide. Before attending I had written to the Director, Salvador, asking him for an invitation (The Hays team in Barcelona is very friendly). I thought it would be much more fun to go with someone, invite a friend. We watched the presentation together, listened attentively to all the speeches (which were very interesting), then afterwards we spent some time talking with the Hays team. Although they were surrounded by people wanting to talk to them, they gave us some of their time. Not only were they extremely friendly, but they also invited us to a series of informative interviews (where you get to know a candidate, but not for a specific position). I came home and felt proud of myself. It was worth it.

The friend I mentioned is a good example of how to manage your contacts. I learnt a lot from her. How I should not be afraid of talking to people, since there is nothing to lose and a whole lot to gain, to name a few of the lessons I learnt. Rule number two is that you need to get out into the real world to meet people. Go to organised events, or anywhere else you think you might meet the right people, such as potential recruiters. You need to get your message heard during your search.

The Key to Networking: Are You Helping Others?

As I mentioned before, managing your contacts is not something you do just when you are searching for a new job; it has to be an integral part of your life.

We meet many people over the course of our life, and some leave more of an impact than others. How we relate to others has an influence on our personal and professional lives. For example, we should always try to catch up with former colleagues after they move on and leave the company. It's always nice to see how friends have succeeded in their new positions or (when they decide to stay) at their existing job. Think about them from time to time, cheer them up when they are down, listen to them if they are struggling with something or simply just enjoy a pleasant time together.

Networking always works best from a positive frame of mind; we are more confident and trusting. Think about it. If you are in the process of changing jobs, then you are going to need someone to confide in about it all. Sharing secrets is about putting yourself out there – a bit like getting naked.

The good news for shy people like me is that networking is a skill that can be learnt and developed. There are some people that seem to have it in their blood, like my friend David, who I mentioned in an earlier chapter. But for others it does not come so naturally. We have to learn how to develop our social skills and relate to people in a satisfying way.

Every chance is a new opportunity to get to know someone. Let me repeat my plane example. Exchanging business cards on planes should be mandatory. How often do you do it? Do you often engage in conversation with strangers, or call or send emails to people you meet at events or by chance? It is important to have a regular network of contacts to rely on throughout the course of your whole life.

A quick example about the importance of meeting people: I once met a very friendly woman, Gizem, on a plane to Istanbul, who worked as a sales professional, and we exchanged cards. I remember her last words to me: "If you need anything from me whilst you are in Turkey, please let me know". I thanked her for her kind words and that was that. But two weeks later, when I was returning to Turkey and thinking about how many problems I'd had with taxi drivers in Istanbul, I thought of her and I asked her if she could recommend a professional car service that could pick me up with a name card whenever needed. And she recommended someone. I could write a whole book on anecdotes about taxi drivers from Istanbul, so I was incredibly grateful for her recommendation. It goes without saying that if there is a time that Gizem asks me for something, I will help her without a doubt. Because when you help someone, they will end up growing to care for you and they will help you back when needed.

If you work on your network constantly, by the time you reach your 40s you will realise that you have an excellent network under your belt. It will have helped you grow professionally, as it would have your contacts, too. And it's great fun stumbling across forgotten contacts when you are carrying out your job searches.

The most important thing is to offer to help your contacts when they need it, and not exclusively in a professional context. Help them with their language skills, or by improving their websites, by sharing your knowledge and experience or simply by having a drink with them and listening to their problems. That is what networking is all about. It is about sharing experiences, camaraderie. The rest comes naturally. After talking with your friends/contacts/acquaintances, they will tell others about how good you are, what your situation is or, even better, how they'd recommend you for a position ("I know the perfect person for that position!"). In fact, at certain executive levels, it is all based on recommendations.

Guide to Accessing Interesting People

If you want to make contact with potential recruiters then you will need a good plan. There are some guidelines that you should follow, such as never disturbing or harassing anyone. Another rule is avoiding direct contact and the sending of unexpectedly long emails. Personally, I hate receiving long emails at work from people I do not know, especially when they do not even contain my name (the standard copy and paste email). The best way to reach out to someone is through an introduction from a mutual contact. If you want to meet someone in particular, check your network of contacts to see if you have any shared contacts who could introduce you. LinkedIn is great for this, since it already suggests intermediary contacts when you view the page of a potential new contact.

As Paulo Coehlo told us in *The Alchemist*, "When you want something, the entire universe conspires in helping you to achieve it.". This philosophy can be applied to your job search. When you begin telling the world that you want to get in touch with a particular company or a person, your contacts will suggest ways for you to reach them. Ask for help. Do not be too proud, we are not alone in this world. You will be surprised at how many interesting people you will meet along the way.

Imagine for a second that you have acquired the email address of someone you want to contact, and you want to write an email. What are you going to say? Stop. Think about the networking guidelines. If you have a shared contact, ask them if they think you should contact them and, if so, what the best way to contact them is (telephone, email, in person...). You should prepare yourself for maybe not getting the answer you want. Or not getting any answer. It is a difficult lesson, but not everybody will want to hear what you have to say or meet up with you. You must respect their decision and not insist.

When you do meet up with someone, be polite; thank them for the opportunity to speak in person; and congratulate them on their achievements. Everyone loves a compliment. However, be direct, too, and do not waste anybody's time ("I am calling because ..."). Introduce yourself well (remember what we covered earlier in the book about presenting yourself). Never directly ask for a job. Instead, explain why you would like to work in a similar company. You are in an interview, of sorts, so make sure you come across as confident. Speak in a calm but firm manner. If the interviewer knows how to drive the conversation, it makes it a lot easier, but if they do not then you will have to lead the way. Do not speak too fast and do not interrupt. If your interviewer does not seem interested, end things well and leave the door open for future potential collaborations. Always leave the door open.

> SUMMARY:
>
> The 10 golden rules for contact management are:
>
> 1. Give out a clear message that you are searching for a job.
> 2. Socialise with people for fun, not because you feel you have to. Choose the people you would like to spend time with.
> 3. Help the others.
> 4. Do not disturb or harass.
> 5. Avoid direct contact, try to be introduced by a mutual contact. .
> 6. Ask your network for help if you need it.
> 7. Be polite at all times.
> 8. Do not waste anybody's time.
> 9. Never directly ask for a work.
> 10. Maintain a regular social life, not just whilst searching for a job.

ADVICE:

I would like to share a summary of things I have learnt during my past job searches:

1.- Things always go better during face-to-face meetings than they do by telephone. (Skype is middle ground). Use the telephone, email or social media to make first contact, since they are powerful tools for this purpose, but once a door has opened, ask to meet for a coffee, lunch or other type of meeting in person. This is especially appreciated when interviewing for recruitment companies. Remember to be brief during telephone calls. People are busy.

2.- The most important thing to consider during a meeting with a contact is whether they feel comfortable and if you are able to find common ground in conversation. When the topic of job hunting comes up in conversation, be direct with what you say:" I am looking for this ", "I need that", "I want to access this company", "I would like to meet that person". Then return to normal conversation. You cannot spend the whole meeting talking about your job hunt.

3.- Networking helps us learn a lot about ourselves. When we open up to our network of contacts, we meet new people - friends of friends and acquaintances of acquaintances. By pushing ourselves out of our comfort zones, we are able to improve how we interact and behave when meeting new people, and discover which topics to focus on or avoid.

4.- Think about it: you are now building your network for the next 10 years. The people you meet will form a part of your network – you will follow them and they will follow you. You might enjoy their posts, seeing how they evolve. You might recommend them for a position and they you in turn. That is the best thing about networking. It is all about building long-lasting relationships.

5.- Do not ask for a job (I have already mention this but it is crucial. Never beg for anything in life, ask for opportunities). We do not know what the impact of our words might be when we approach a potential new contact. The contact may decide not to connect as they feel you are there to take advantage of them, for example. However, on the flipside, we might make a positive impact just by mentioning out current situation, profile and activities.

6.- Things are much easier if we do what we really want to do, or what we do well. Begin networking by joining in activities that you feel comfortable with - your hobbies. Be yourself as much as you can. This makes everything much easier. I discovered that I was much better at managing my contacts if they were people I felt I had something in common with. Obviously, we cannot control what topics might come up, and it is good to be exposed to people with opposing opinions, positive or negative, but you can choose how open you are with each other.

7.- **Important: always focus on your end goal**, since opportunities arise when you least expect them.

8.- **You're job hunting so keep an eye out for related events or activities**. Events will help you meet people. Attend conferences, presentations, networking sessions, and after-work events (very popular these days). Whilst at these events, remember to be extremely polite and exchange business cards so you can follow up and thank them for their time the following day.

9.- **Being aggressive is a mistake.** You can *burnout* a contact very quickly by being too pushy, insistent or annoying. You should only be very direct in those situations where there is no other option, and being aware of the possibility that you might lose the contact. If you are close friends, then you can get to the point: "Could you to introduce me to such and such".

However, this should be the only exception to the rule. Be relaxed and ready to meet new people. Wait for them to introduce you to other people, so you can continue to build your network.

10.- Listen carefully to the needs of others. And help them out expecting nothing in return. Networking means relating with other people. The best way to become integrated in a community is by offering your services and helping out others.

How to Use Social Media to Your Advantage

Twitter

If you are looking for a job, Twitter can be a very useful tool. From my own experience, I can share the following advice:

1.- **Open a separate account from your personal account** and use it exclusively for job searches. Twitter is very interactive and you might get distracted by your friends if you are already a regular user. Focus on job searches. Your time on Twitter must be effective and productive.

2.- **Follow recruitment consultants on Twitter**. Use the search filters and keywords to locate them ("recruiter", "headhunter", "job search" etc.). The more specialised they are in a certain sector, the better for you (i.e. specific recruiters for the retail sector, banking, etc.). If you know the names of those you wish to contact then search for them directly.

3.- **Carry out specific searches on Twitter for your desired positions**. For example, search for "Finance Director",

"Key Account Manager for Aerospace", etc., as per your desired position. Relevant job postings will appear in your search results. Click onto the profiles of those people who like or Retweet the relevant posts, since they could be searching for a job like you, work as a recruiter or have links to job hunting newsletters or magazines. Look at the timelines of people of interest.

4.- **Be goal oriented**. Keep it simple and do not overload yourself with information. If, for example, you are following a recruiter from a different sector, unfollow them, as you want your timeline to reflect 100% relevant information. Avoid white noise on your timeline.

5.- **Leave the door open to receive emails and notifications** from Twitter, as they could suggest similar profiles or positions. Social media is much more advanced these days and Twitter can do a lot of the work for you now.

6.- **Follow companies that you would like to work for**. Interact with them (offering intelligent and useful comments). Not only will it help you keep on top of their vacancies, but also it will keep you better informed of their strategies, results and new products, etc.

7.- Try to meet professionals like you (I-Meet). Do a simple search by position or sector to find people like you. Check out Twitter's "similar people" or "people related to".

8.- Try to meet professionals like you. (II- Interact). Ration your time on Twitter. Focus on the people that you follow. Thank those that follow you and post interesting comments (if you feel happy posting), but try to keep all other communication to a minimum. Twitter is just a platform to get you where you need to be: a part of your networking strategy.

9.- Be a proactive user. Post interesting comments and the rest will follow.

10.- Be honest with the information that you share. Remember this is part of your personal brand. People create an image of who you are through what you write. It is all about image.

LinkedIn

As with most real life situations, LinkedIn comes with a set of guidelines. Not so long ago I saw a message on LinkedIn, posted by a top CEO, stating, "Before writing to me, ask yourself if you really know me in real". The first golden rule on LinkedIn is to be careful with how you present yourself!!

Most people are friendly and receptive during an initial contact. Nevertheless, one must always be careful with the limits of respect and privacy. If you would not write a direct email to someone you do not know, then why would you contact him or her directly through LinkedIn? Especially considering this contact request is likely to generate an email in their personal email account anyway.

When I was a global executive at a multinational company, I had very little free time and too many emails to read each day as it was, so I wasn't very receptive to emails from strangers. Any email sent to my professional address without a mention of a mutual contact, usually ended up in my Trash folder. I never accepted contact requests through LinkedIn unless I first received a short, friendly introduction. On the other hand, if I wanted to give someone a chance, I would accept the contact request and await further contact. If contact were not made within a couple of weeks then I would delete them. I swear I actually wrote this in my plan. Delete them.

Because I like to pride myself on maintaining my LinkedIn contacts up to date, making sure that I am acquainted with all my "contacts". I only have one exception to this rule: when people contact me because they like something I have written on my blog. I can respect this. But there still has to be some kind of emails interchange between us. Some people, like me, take LinkedIn very seriously so try to respect others as much as possible.

My recommendations for LinkedIn are therefore:

- **Get introduced**. Being introduced to a third party at a bar is not the same as walking up to them with drink in hand to introduce yourself. If you have a mutual contact (who can at least inform your LinkedIn contact in advance) then the whole process is so much easier.

- **Friendship requests are a good way to get to know people**, if you do not have access to LinkedIn's paid *In Mails* feature (direct messaging between users). But do it right. Add a few lines to the request message, such as, "I am writing to you in reference to...", "May I borrow 5 minutes of your time ...", "I would love to add you to my network...", etc. Something personal. If you are recommended by a mutual friend things go much easier always.

- **Be gentle with your language**. Imagine yourself in the *Palais de Versailles* during the XIX Century, or in Victorian London on your way to a ball. Using colloquial language on LinkedIn can sometimes come across as rude or aggressive. Show maximum respect at all times.

- **LinkedIn is not (yet) Facebook**. Though the platforms have their similarities such as the newsfeed timelines, try not to comment too much on posts you see, especially if you are expressing personal opinions. Though I know of many friends who do this, do keep in mind that posting too often on LinkedIn could be assimilated to having too little work or too much free time. I belong to a generation that believes that the use of social media platforms at the office is a bad thing. Luckily, Millennials have changed this view, since they are hyper-connected at all times. Moreover, some of us use LinkedIn to access potential customers/suppliers.

- **LinkedIn creates a profile of your personality and personal branding**. More than any other social network. By congratulating people on their birthdays, commenting on people's promotions and interacting in a friendly manner, you are creating a profile full of personality.

- **Link your profile to your sector**. The personality you promote through your LinkedIn profile can extend to your professional sector. Participate in relevant forums and write about your profession. It is a great way to gain visibility, although visibility is pointless if you are not already interacting with your contacts.

- **Lately, LinkedIn is allowing public posts**. Treat it like a blog, but remember there is an audience. This feature is only recommended for experienced *bloggers*. Starting from zero as a LinkedIn *blogger* can be risky.

- **LinkedIn helps people connect with people** by recommending *people you might already know,* as with other social media platforms. It reminds you of upcoming birthdays, notifies you when someone is promoted, etc. It encourages people to get in touch with each other. Take them up on their offer.

Finally, remember to keep on top of your LinkedIn network. Focus your efforts on developing relationships with potential contacts in the real world. Maintaining contacts for the sake of it is a waste of everybody's time.

Chapter 6: The Interview

Interview Preparation

You should never go to an interview without preparing beforehand, just as you should never go to an exam without having studied. Even though it might just be an informative interview, where a recruitment company or headhunter is interested in finding out more about you, you still must be fully prepared.

Sometimes I think back to some of the interviews I attended when I was younger. They would ask me (I smile when I think back to this): "Could you please tell me about any achievements gained through previous experience?". Since I was not ready for that question, I responded with an "Mmmmm..." and tried to think on my feet. In the end, I am sure the example I gave was good enough, but it was incredibly improvised because it had not occurred to me to prepare for that type of question. I was so naive!

There are certain questions in an interview that you can prepare for. Of course, you could just improvise, but there is no comparison with a well-prepared, structured and concise response, that has been rehearsed and well-explained

We are now going to look at 10 simple steps for preparing for a job interview:

1. **Read the job description carefully.** If you do not have it to hand, ask for a copy, or for more information on the position. You should know what the company is looking for, and most job postings include a brief description of the company and position. Think about what type of company it is, who you will be reporting to, if you will be managing a team, how technical the position is, and what skills are required. Treat the job description as if it were your *Bible* and, much like the Bible, refer back to it when you are not sure how to move forward.

2. **Investigate the company profile.** You need to learn about the place where you might end up working. I think there are two things to consider here: the company's mission and its values. You should empathise, or at least feel comfortable with, the company. Then find out what financial situation the company is in by looking up relevant financial reports (often available through the company website). The company profile is going to have an influence on your

decision. It is one thing to work in a company that is in the process of expansion, quite another to work in one that is reducing its workforce. The next step is to research the company and its various subsidiaries, customer references, etc. Start thinking about similar companies and products that you have collaborated with to provide relevant examples.

3. **Complement your company research with extra details.** It helps to get to know the company from the inside. You can find a lot of information through Wikipedia, for example, including links to top companies (as a start). Other companies publish information through their websites. Read online articles. Try to establish who's who in the company. Look at your network of contacts for people already working there or people able to put you in touch with someone at the company. Every little helps.

4. **Do you really want this position?** Now that you have enough information, be honest with yourself and ask yourself this question: if you really want to work at that company and in that position. Whilst writing this, I am remembering a recruitment process that I walked away from once, after finding out how the company work internally and hearing negative feedback from people working there. If the

same thing happens to you, it's OK. Just be polite and explain why you will be leaving the process, then go. Remember one my favourite quotes: Never waste time or waste the time of others. Better now than further down the line.

5. **Analyse your experience well**. Now you need to prepare your profile, starting by adjusting your technical knowledge so it is in line with the job description. I believe this is a good point, using all the information you have gathered about yourself, to begin working on your elevator pitch – a two-minute presentation about who you are. The answer to the question: could you please introduce yourself? Here you should adapt your examples to the requirements of the position.

6. **Analyse your abilities.** Every position requires specific abilities. They might be managerial or they might be more technical, social or uniquely specific. This part is difficult to prepare (perhaps the hardest part of preparing for an interview). Not everyone is a great leader, a sociable and dynamic person, or an entrepreneur. You must understand here that there is no standard answer. You just need to prepare this part with as much honesty and self-awareness as possible , just as you did when writing your CV.

7. **Personal questions.** Now that you have prepared the more technical aspects of the interview, your abilities, we can move on to personal information. It is common to be asked about your personal life. This information might include personal achievements and professional failures. Success is easy to prepare for, but normally one is not ready to speak about failures. A failure could be a project that failed during launch. In this example, you would need to explain the context surrounding the failure, and what you learnt from the experience. Because we all make mistakes, but not all of us can learn from them. That requires a certain degree of self-criticism and a desire to learn. Keep your answers simple: "After that project we learnt a valuable lesson on how standardising the four key activities crucial for a project launch".

8. **Dress code.** First impressions can *impress* or disappoint, and every position has its *look*. We cannot ignore the fact that we are selling an image, and first impressions tend to stick. Dress in accordance with the position you apply for. There is a big difference between applying for a Commercial Director position, and applying for one as an Advertising Copywriter. Some companies take it more seriously than others, but there is always a dress code. It is also important that you feel comfortable and relaxed in what you are

wearing. Don't wear anything too flashy or excessively casual. Wear something that helps you forget that you are attending an interview. Shoes should always be clean, as cleanliness always works in your favour. Adjust your wardrobe according to company and position profiles. I am laughing as I write this, because I remember giving this advice to my brother before he interviewed for his current job, and I also told him to wear a white shirt with long sleeves to cover his tattoos. He followed my advice. However, in the middle of the interview, he rolled up his sleeves because it was warm in the room and they saw some of his tattoos. And they love them! It's a *start-up*, the atmosphere is very relaxed, and they really value creativity and diversity. They told him that they offered him the job, not just because of his profile, but because he seemed a good fit for the corporate culture.

9. **During the interview**. Always look your interviewer in the eye and do not focus on just one person if there is more than one interviewer. Be proactive with your answers, but do not embellish too much. Simply show interest and smile, always smile. Try to visualise yourself in the position. I know someone who has always worked as a receptionist, and at a glance you can tell immediately (calm voice, good manners, etc.). Behave in line with the expectations of the position throughout your interview.

10. **After the interview**. Be polite. Be gentle and charming. Thank them for the interview and the time they dedicated to you and your profile. You can call or write to show interest, but these processes can be slow so it is always better to do it in person.

Finally, I must insist that the most important thing to remember is to be yourself during the interview.

Weaknesses

I have noticed that there is a crucial factor when preparing for an interview that many people do not take into consideration: awareness of your weaknesses. For example, I get very nervous before an interview. Any type of interview. With age, I have learnt to be less nervous and anxious. I sometimes pinch myself to try to calm those initial nerves and distract myself until I become fully immersed in the interview and I am able to relax. I cannot avoid being shy, but I can control my nerves and make sure the interviewer is not aware of them.

Let's look at another type of weakness. For me, a weakness is any insecurity that can be quickly detected in an interview. The biggest insecurities tend to derive from the question: Why did you leave your last job? Often the candidate gets nervous and starts a story, generally a long one, which leads to more questions as the interviewer begins to doubt their nervous response. Whilst you are reeling off your story, you lose face in front of the interviewer and begin to lose confidence in yourself.

Simple and brief answers can be prepared for difficult questions, but insecurities need a bit more attention. There is a lot to be said about insecurity, and the line between insecurity and obsession is a fine one. Many people become obsessed after a negative experience such as being fired from a long-term job, and it takes them a long time to get over it. Some people even start crying when they broach the subject (I have seen it with my own eyes). In my modest opinion, one must decide to what extent we will allow insecurity to control us, before getting back on the road to recovery. The sooner you deal with it (with expert help if needed) the better, so that you can get on with the business of interviewing.

I once helped a man, Edward, to find a job. One of his fears was that he did not have enough previous experience using particular administrative software. This software was very much in demand. He was very worried about it, so we dedicated quite a bit of time to seeing how we could overcome the obstacle. In the end, he decided it would be a good idea to spend a few days with some colleagues who used the same software often. When we talked again he commented that it had been much easier than he'd imagined to use it, and that now he could face interviews in the knowledge that, if asked, he could say he had used the software at work at a beginner level. The main thing was that he turned a weakness into strength.

I hear many common insecurities through my job: "I am way too old to find a job", "I've been out of the job market for too long", to name a few. The worst part was that there was an element of truth to what they were saying .It is true that the market discriminates by age, but the opposite could be said, too: someone who is qualified can find a job regardless of age. The good news is that a good recruiter will look much further than age and focus on the person and their talents. So, in a sense, we are all at a slight competitive disadvantage, but if we are able to cancel this out with motivation and our skills and abilities, then it makes no difference. Think about how you could compensate these disadvantages. Keep things in perspective and find a way to turn your insecurities into strengths. That is all there is to it.

In my case (and I have not told many people this), until not so long ago I had a fear of being asked about my private life and being rejected for not fitting into the profile of an executive. It is socially pre-assumed that an executive has to be married with children. However, this is not true. A single and very happy person can also be a good executive and professional overall. Now I have a well-rehearsed 30 second answer to this question, and I am not worried about ruining an interview because of my response. It's gone from being an insecurity to being a part of my profile. Some insecurities are based on fears and assumptions, and others are based on personal factors; how we see ourselves (or how we think others see us). There is nothing much to it except to accept who we are and what we are like. When talking about it with two ex-bosses, they confessed to me that they had thought about it during interviews but then decided it was neither appropriate nor relevant to the position. They were more interested in my professional experience and not in my personal life.

Ultimately, what is the worst thing that could happen? That they ask you a politically incorrect question? Let me tell you about a real case that I will never forget. It involves a former university colleague. She was attending an interview for a trainee position at a car manufacturing plant. At that time, we all wanted to do our post university practical training at THE CAR MANUFACTURING PLANT. They asked her an awkward question about being a woman and questioned what her expectations of life were. She became our class hero by responding with: "If you did not want to hire a woman, then why did you invite me to this interview?" The interviewer apologised, but the damage had been done and neither of them wanted to work together. Luckily, times have changed since the nineties and most companies these days would not risk missing out on talent because of someone's gender (she's a senior executive these days).

Let's focus on how to combat these insecurities. Start with the old saying that there is an advantage for every disadvantage; So, in the example of "I am too old", why not instead say "I am an experienced person and I am going to demonstrate it during my interview". Instead of being afraid that "They'll think I am too proud and a "know it all"", think, "I am a secure person that transmits security to others during an interview", and so on. It is very important to get to know our fears and limitations, and to be able to turn them on their heels and convert them into strengths. That is what the SWOT analysis we saw before is all about, and it is the most important part of your search. Concentrate on the positive aspects whilst preparing for an interview; reinforce your strengths and give it your best. You will have no more than an hour to demonstrate that you are qualified to do the job, so there is no time to waste on weaknesses. Provide quick and brief answers and, above all, act natural.

I must warn you at this point: be careful with being honest about your language skills. I speak fluent German and once, during a break whilst conducting a shared interview, a colleague from Human Resources told me to ask the candidate the following, in German: "how do you cope with pressure and what do you do when things don't go to plan at work?" So I asked the candidate and his answer confirmed what we had suspected. When speaking a foreign language, we tend to relax and control our thoughts less. By asking him a question in a foreign language, it acted like a truth serum and he answered sincerely without thinking. Be careful.

How to Prepare for a Job Interview in One Afternoon

Sometimes things escalate and they call you when you least expect it. They liked your CV and they are impatient to meet you. They think you would be a perfect fit for the job and they want to introduce you to your future employer who is in between flights at the moment. He or she has a free slot... tomorrow!

So you have less than one afternoon to prepare for your interview. Where do you start? Well, first thing's first, you need to lock yourself away at home or in your office (anywhere really so long as it is quiet and you can be alone), then read your CV out loud and rehearse your standard interview answers. Put some relaxing music on to create a relaxing atmosphere. Now quickly review your CV and tell yourself who are you. Do not follow your CV word for word. Instead, explain your different paths: how you came to be here, where you started from and what motivates you.

Create your elevator pitch, and then expand on it with your own story. If you lack inspiration at any time or feel blocked, stop and review. Maybe that is the area that you need to address in order to create a better description. Think about what happened before and after, but do not waste time if you cannot see a way to move forward. If you are able to describe your CV well then you have 20% of the interview covered. If you are still struggling, do not worry: you might think of something in the shower tomorrow.

Once you have finished reviewing your CV, start analysing the job description. Are you a good fit? What new functions can you see? What similar functions have you done before? Help merge your CV with the position being offered by including examples and similar situations in your descriptions to demonstrate your skills and abilities. That's another 20% of the interview covered. That is 40% so far.

Now we get to the importance part: *fulfilling expectations*. Imagine you are a potential recruiter. What would you expect from a candidate, and how should they behave? For example, a Quality Director is expected to be serious and respectful with timings, as well as being resolute and having an eye for detail (amongst other things). A Quality Director from the fashion industry (retail, for example) is also expected to have knowledge of different fabrics and products (clothes and patterns). Speak in terms of competences (Directiveness) and skills (knowledge of the sector/function/product and quality). If you do not possess both, then focus on your strengths and demonstrate motivation for what you lack. That is another 20% (you have prepared 60% of the interview, now).

Everything else is just about being motivated. Ask yourself if you really want the position. If it fits into your career path. If you can grow as a professional in the company. If it aligns with your professional trajectory. If there is potential for growth in the company then think about WHY there is. This "why" is your motivational weapon. Start the interview with a phrase such as "I want to work in this company because…" or "this position motivates me because…." If you cannot motivate yourself, do not go to the interview. Another 30% done (we are up to 90% now).

The remaining 10% (percentages are a guide, of course) is all about YOU. Think about who you are. Often, recruiters choose a candidate because of who they are over their technical experience. Skills can be learnt or transferred. When it comes to this part of the interview, answer all questions politely and in a positive way. Above all, show them that you are motivated!

Get Your Job Interview off to a Good Start

I always compare attending a job interview with playing at a concert. You get nervous and excited with anticipation because you know that you'll be getting the chance to reach many people who are going to evaluate your talent. So, much like singers or musicians, we need to have a few tricks up our sleeve to make sure the interview goes off to a good start. The first few minutes are crucial when it comes to leaving a lasting impression. If that impression is bad, then it will be difficult to change their opinion after.

The first thing you need to have under control is the technical aspect of the interview. There's no time to lose so, for example, check Skype addresses and Wi-Fi connections for long distance interviews, in advance. The same goes for conference call numbers. Take it from me after many years of starting conference meetings late because participants do not show up on time. Do not make people anxious by keeping them waiting. Most of my executive friends are like me, with some exceptions, but even these exceptions make an effort to connect on time for special occasions.

You need to find the right balance, the middle ground between being motivated and being arrogant, whilst maintaining an interest in the company. During an interview, it is assumed that the candidate has taken the time to look at the corporate website whilst researching the company. So do not say "I have visited the website and I know the company well", "I know all about the company" or "I know you work in this way or that way". It is a little unnerving being told about your own company by an interview candidate. I know through experience. One must be very subtle and discreet, feed them pieces of information so they can converse with you in a natural way. And if you want to express motivation and optimism: "I see the company is expanding... What's your secret?" If you have any technical questions, mention that you will save them for the end of the interview.

Obviously, it all depends on how well you bond with your interviewer, but prudence never hurts anyone. Questions that do not have any direct bearing on your interview should be avoided (such as the finer details of the position, the internal organisation of the company, next steps after the interview, etc.). Leave these questions for later. If there is information you feel is important to know i.e. who you will report to, do not hesitate to enquire and then prepare your subsequent answers accordingly. I always appreciate candidates who express an interest but I also implore them to save their questions for the last 5 minutes of the interview (which I always reserve for this purpose).

One of the biggest mistakes you can make is not listening enough at the start of an interview. Not all interviews include a detailed and complete presentation of the company and the position at the start. But if it does, all the better! It is a gift to the candidate. Not only will it provide you with information missed during your interview preparation, but it will also allow you to complete your profiles for the company and position. Furthermore, it will help you evaluate whether you see yourself in the role and working at the company, since the interviewer is making you feel a part of the company already. Most of us tend to imagine ourselves at the company and position before the interview. This visualisation can have a positive and a negative effect (a shock if it is not what you expected). In both cases, try to find relevant examples from your past experience.

All of this is crucial for giving you the best start in the interview. Prepare well for your interviews, as you would for any other meeting.

What Does Ego Have to Do with Your Interview?

The ego can be very disruptive to an interview. It can ruin it if you let it. Let's look at some examples.

I have a healthy dose of self-esteem and I have always felt proud of myself, but during an interview for a position in Munich once, it was so clear that I was the right candidate for the job that I became completely involved in the role and answered every question as if I already worked there. Suddenly the interviewer asked me: Why are you so proud of yourself? (Warum bist du so stolz? Everything sounds sterner in German). I remember giving an apporpiate answer (I am told I am good at maintaining my cool and being calm and mild mannered), but things were tense. There was a clash of egos. I probably came across as being quite arrogant and from my perspective, I felt as if I had been judged on just one impression for the whole of my profile. That day I learnt that I could only sing an aria at the right point of the opera, not sing the aria at the start without being requested so.

Another mistake is not respecting the ego of your interviewer by, for example, not looking everyone in the eye when being interviewed by multiple managers or directors, instead maintain eye contact with the most senior member of staff only, forgetting about who will be their reporting manager. Big mistake! The direct manager has a strong weight in the decisions, and if they feel ignored and disrespected as a manager then they will find an excuse not to hire you. Worst-case scenario, if the big boss really liked you and puts pressure on other staff to hire you, then there is a big chance you will be seen as a threat by many. These small mistakes can have severe consequences for your interview. So relax your ego, and do not expect to go for a coffee with the CEO after your interview.

The ego also emerges when there is an opportunity for the candidate to display interest in the company, as mentioned before. It is good to show interest through comments such as "I have seen online that you are developing new products. I find that very interesting". This massages the ego of the interviewer and provides you with added value since you have shown both knowledge and interest. But try to avoid a clash of egos; an "I know more than you" battle. Be humble, ask for information and, above all, try to make a connection with your interviewer.

Another important point is that you should never interrupt your interviewer, no matter how keen you are to express your point of view or respond to a question. No matter how quickly your mind starts racing, be patient and always let people finish what they have to say. An interview is like being in a cafe with someone: it requires good listening skills. However, being humble does not mean being passive. Overly submissive candidates are rarely favoured. You need to impress your interviewer and live up to the expectations of the job.

There is another aspect that I always insist on: spontaneity. This includes explaining your CV in a natural way, the way you do it best. Nobody wants to listen to an overly rehearsed script (I have seen candidates read from a text). Be yourself. If a company does not take you on, there will be others. Good interviewers will see you as a whole, even if you did provide weaker answers than other candidates did.

Keep a positive attitude at all times. This is expected from candidates above everything else, regardless of what mistakes you might have made. I come from a Latin/Catholic culture, centred on blame and punishment, so I have learnt a lot whilst working with Belgians and the Dutch. Their cultures are not so condemning of errors. In fact, they openly discuss them. They accept the consequences and apply the lessons they have learnt to future activities and projects. I follow these principles to the letter during my day-to-day life, especially the part about LEARNING. This is what I expect from a candidate - the capacity to learn and not have a meltdown in moments of stress. If you have had an issue at work, do not beat yourself up. Think about what you have learnt, how you managed the problem so it would not happen again, and which processes you standardised afterwards. This competence is greatly valued by companies at management level. To conclude, it is pointless trying to cover up your mistakes. It is better to face them head on, remedy them quickly, and then learn from the experience.

The best interviews are those that have the feel of sharing a coffee together. Where space and time lose their meaning and your interview goes on for well over the (expected) hour. The best interviews are those where all the right questions are asked, and the ones that allow you to get straight to the essence of who you are. The best interviews are definitely those where you are able to clearly express yourself, in a positive and motivated manner.

Difficult Questions

Recruiters always want to make sure that they hire the best possible candidate, so they like to turn it up a notch and challenge candidates with difficult questions during an interview. Sometimes it is done to see how candidates react in a certain situation, and sometimes they are just pushing for additional information. You cannot take it personally or overthink it. Respond to these questions in a calm, structured way, including any difficult questions.

There are two types of difficult question. Firstly, there are difficult personal questions, which we have already spoken about (family status, personality, etc.). Secondly, there are those related to the professional world and complicated work-based relations. The latter are much harder to prepare for. We are aware of our personal issues but we do not often stop to analyse why we did such and such at our previous job.

Let us start with the personal side of things. One thing I am asked on a regular basis at my workshops (especially by women) is how to balance your work and home life. Wait a few seconds before responding, and look at your interviewer. If you think they might be working a 70-80 hour week then do not mention how important balancing your work and home is. I know it is not very politically correct, but this is reality. I am a big fan of having a healthy work/home balance, but I admit that it can be difficult to achieve in practice. In the majority of new jobs, especially management ones, you would need to be completely dedicated for at least the first six months. If you have just had a baby, you will not see him/her much over the next few months, so maybe it is not the best point to launch a new career, be promoted or change jobs. There will be plenty of time later down the line though. Never lose sight of your end goal.

If, for example, you are asked if you would be available to travel, remember that honesty is an important asset. They are probably asking you this because people often say that it is not a problem, and then afterwards they are full of excuses. I have seen it twice during my own career as a manager, where the position required travelling and the candidate did not comply, despite confirming it would not be a problem during the interview.

The best advice for questions such as these is to be honest and clear with your interviewer. I know a couple of people who have rejected positions because they considered the travel requirements of the job to be excessive (more than 3 days a week) and they thought it would not be compatible with their family commitments. Their honesty was respected and nobody doubted their professionalism. Better to be honest in advance than accept conditions that you are not able to abide by. Ultimately, it is your life, but you need to be upfront and honest whatever you do.

These days it is much easier to reconcile your work and home life. My advice is to be honest and defend your professionalism. You can give examples in the interview such as, "I have no problem visiting the production site AT THE START of my contract". Continue with a "AFTER THAT I will coordinate my trips through continuous communication with the sites and always under your supervision".

Moving on to personal matters, be aware that your life it is your life and you do not have to hide anything. Being a man/woman/immigrant/married /with or without children is who you are. Explain, in a positive way, how you believe yourself to be capable for the job independently of your home and work life. Recruiters appreciate small concessions, though. If you have two children and your partner is able to pick them up from school, you will be in a much better position to negotiate that overtime or those five o'clock meetings. In any case, never lie about your circumstances or intentions. What counts is showing empathy towards your interviewer and the company. From an interviewer's point of view, it is difficult to understand when a candidate starts negotiating terms before they have even been offered a position at the company.

Although you should not shy away from personal questions, it is a good idea to establish some limits. I do. If I do not think a question is relevant to the position, or I think it is better suited to a friendly meeting in a pub, then I am very blunt in my response. I answer on a Yes/No basis. If the topic continues, I will say, "I don't think this is relevant to the position". Some people might not like this answer, since it displays temperament, which might result in them feeling rejected. Avoid being too stern, it costs nothing to explain things in detail. But be yourself. Remember, if they are questioning you in this way in an interview, it is only going to get worse if you get the job. Sometimes we have to define and defend our own limits.

The final aspect to prepare for, and be able to defend, is any gaps in your professional timeline. You will always be questioned about it. "Why did you change from A to B?" or "I see here that you spent a year unemployed". People are often worried about these questions and interviewers worry about what candidate's answers might be. Prepare a brief and clear response for each gap or move in your career. The goal here is to satisfy your interviewer's curiosity. There is no need to provide a detailed answer. We are not here to speak about the past (especially if it was not even due to your actions, as is often the case), just the future. Do not waste more time than needed on questions of this type.

In the following table, you will find a list of difficult questions. Many of them have been designed for a better understanding of your management style during difficult situations. It is important to accept your mistakes, and it is even more important to learn from them and take something positive from the experience. If relevant, include data, percentages, detailed descriptions, examples and background in order to help your interviewer understand your answers.

Question	Don't say	Recommended response
What have you been doing throughout your two years of unemployment?	"I have been actively job hunting"	"I have combined active job hunting with building on my experiences by…" Add any experiences related to teaching, charity work, associations that you have joined. Show activity
Why did you leave your last company?	The blunt truth with a dramatic explanation.	The official version agreed with your company. Do not waste precious interview time on this topic. It is a common question, so make sure you prepare an answer. Remember, they can always double check by

Question	Don't	Recommended response
		using your provided references.
Tell me three positive and three negative aspects about you.	Be too critical about yourself, show negativity or go into too much detail.	Negative points could relate to a different sector, for example. Or something small like you were not aware of all products. These are minor disadvantages.
Describe briefly how you see your career developing over the next 5 years.	"I would like to be a boss" or "I would like to have your job" (although the interviewer might take it with good humour and answer you: "you'd have to kill me first").	I see myself helping a department grow as an effect of my contributions" or "I hope to be able to help my manager grow, too. That we can help each other grow". You could also say that you want to improve your knowledge and use it to contribute to the success of the company. (not everybody wants a professional career)
Give me an example of a failed project and how you	Focus too much on the technical and negative aspects.	A short explanation (prepared and rehearsed at home). Focus on the lessons learnt, what

dealt with it.		improvements you developed off the back of it, and how you ensured it did not happen again. Believe what you are saying and transmit the feeling to your interviewer.
Question	Don't	Recommended response
When was the last time you failed to share your Manager's opinion, and why did you disagree?	Disagreeing with a Manager is a form of confrontation (mentally). Never bypass your manager and go to his/her boss.	Good companies look for criticism from their employees, but also from those that are able to express it through analysis, data, provided said criticism directly relates to the good of the company. Explain the situation to your boss and outline the options, leaving the final decision to your boss.
I see there is a possibility that you are overqualified for the position.	"Well maybe.....but.."	There's no such thing as being under or over qualified for a position. What matters is how motivated you are and if you do things well. If you

		have made it to the interview stage then it is because they saw something in you. Stick to your guns and defend your candidacy if you are, indeed, overqualified.
Question	Don't say	Recommended response
Why do you want to work in this company?	"Everybody knows that this company is leading the market". "I like the company, and I think I'd enjoy working here and I'd be a good fit". This is the standard answer they are expecting to hear. There is no benefit from your perspective.	NEUTRAL OPTION: "I would like to learn from your company, as I know you are leading the market. I want to internalise the corporate values and contribute to its success. MOTIVATED OPTION: "I want to help this company grow by applying all my abilities as ... and I guarantee you will get the best of me".
Do you have any questions?	"Do you manufacture that product?" "What are company revenues like?" "Do you have sites at X	Start a conversation by posing interesting questions: ORGANISATION/ POSITION OPTION.: "I

	country?"	am interested in finding out how the department is distributed. How you deal with this or that in this company".
		PRODUCT OPTION: "I have seen online that you are developing a new range of products relating to this field...", "What do you think about the technology of the future...", "Will that product continue to be developed?", etc...

Typical Interview Mistakes

I have explained this before, but I really must insist on how important it is not to read anything during an interview. Watch out with Skype interviews. It is very amusing to see a candidate reading a text during a Skype call, but it is not in the candidate's favour, and it does not say much about their improvisation skills.

Another thing, which I find amusing (I like encountering unexpected situations on Skype) is when, whilst talking with a candidate who is at their home, a friend, family member or cleaner appears at the other end of the room. It can be very distracting, though, and it stops me from fully reading the candidate. I will normally make a comment to the candidate, since it is an interruption, after all. Although I might find it amusing, it usually results in them losing Brownie points.

A big, common mistake is not calculating how long your answers will take. The interviewer probably has a list of questions to cover. If they stumble across a personal interest, then they will probably want to discuss it further. One hour is the standard duration of an interview, but a good interview could last up to an hour and a half if both sides are motivated to continue. I always conduct interviews with candidates outside of regular office hours and, knowing what I am like, I will probably have dinner or attend to personal appointments or scheduled meetings after the interview. I usually prepare my questions in advance, so no matter how much I like the candidate, if they exceed the time limit for each question, I'll start getting nervous as I realise I will be late for my next appointment, and this can sometimes mean I don't focus on the answers as much as I should. However, the worst situation is when a candidate answers with an inappropriate or overtly long response, providing too much information. I normally drop a few hints but sometimes people do not react to them or modify what they are saying. I am sorry, but when this happens, I totally disconnect from the interview, which is the worst thing that could happen. Conclusion: Only communicate what is required and slow down so the interviewer can process all the information.

Negotiating Your Salary During the Recruitment Process

At a certain point of the process, you will be asked for your salary expectations. It could be at the very beginning of the recruitment process, through the Recruitment Company or headhunter, or during one of the interviews. It goes without saying that the higher the position is, the sooner they will ask. They do this because some executives are not willing to make a commitment towards getting a new job at a company if there is no financial reward motivating it. There are some salary bands that immediately remove a candidate from the process.

What happens, then, if, you are asked about your salary expectations during your first interview? Obviously, you have to prepare this question well. You need to have firm knowledge of the market and know where you fit in on the scale (higher or lower range salary). You need to know how much you are worth (objectively speaking) and how much the market would be willing to pay for you. Hays Executive regularly publishes updated salary ranges by position, sector, and years of experience. Have a look. It could be useful.

When they ask you for a figure, never give a specific number. Open it to a maximum and a minimum value that you would accept. Ultimately, you will have to meet somewhere in the middle. Mention the word "estimate" and leave the door open for negotiations. You do not want to lose an opportunity because you have talked about money too soon (if you are motivated to get the position). By doing this, you are being clear about your expectations, and you can always reject the job if the salary does not meet them.

It is important to remember that nothing is final until the process has ended, and always wait for a company to make you a firm offer. Give them some margins and respect their timings for discussing salaries. Some companies consider it inappropriate to discuss salaries at too early a stage. Money is important but sometimes it is less important than finding the RIGHT PERSON. I am not going to explain negotiation tactics to you here, although I love to negotiate, (it would be long and there are already many books on the topic). I will tell you, though, that everything has its price and you need to evaluate how much you are worth, not just based on what you have done in the past, but also on what you will do in the future. From here, you will be able to ascertain if your expectations match what's being offered. Think about it. Whether or not the company accepts your maximum range, if you are asking for more than the competition, for example, it would be difficult to justify an increase. On the other hand, I know cases where people have been looking for a position for over three years and the company needed to hire a candidate, so they ended up paying what the candidate wanted.

Another option is to negotiate a starting salary which, after six months and provided the company is satisfied, will be subject to a raise (with a pre-signed agreement when you start at the company). Unfortunately, I have seen many situations where this agreement was not adhered to, at surprising levels and with hard working people. I am more of a "bird in the hand..." kind of person. I give it my all, and then wait to see what happens.

I like to be well-paid and I like the people working for me to be well-paid, too. Therefore, I always strive for high salaries. This is not a bad thing, but you must consider your own limitations. As Napoleon once said, it is better to have a timely withdrawal than lose the battle. Think of this as a general rule once you are in the company. It is difficult to get a raise, but it is not impossible if you perform well. Sometimes companies would rather keep you satisfied in terms of salary, than have you leave the company. Think about how long you expect to be at this company and if you are able to accept a salary reduction knowing that you will be paid more at your next job after learning the ropes. In conclusion, it is very important to get to know yourself, the market and your competition in the sector you are approaching.

ADVICE

If you really like a specific position, do not withdraw from the process for salary reasons before visiting the company and meeting with your potential future boss. Sometimes compromises can be met, and money is not everything in life. The company may decide to re-evaluate their offer if they cannot find anyone suitable with the lower salary band offered.

Think about it. If you are much lower than the market, it will only be a matter of time before the company is forced to increase your salary to stop competitors from tempting you away. Keep the position in perspective and look at the bigger picture.

Chapter 7: After the Interview

When It's Not You

Let's imagine that the interview has gone well and you are feeling positive about things. What happens now?

It might seem like all the hard work has been done once you have attended an interview, but this is not the case. There is still a bit of work required in terms of follow up. In addition, regardless of whether or not you fell in love with the company or their management style, you still need to find out everything you can about the company. Find out about the internal structure by speaking to people already working there and resolve any doubts you might still have. You have probably done all, if not most, of this whilst preparing for your interview, but knowing someone in the company already with whom you could discuss your interview could be interesting (provided they left the door open for future communication). . It is good to have an objective contact also, though. Not only will they give you a fresh perspective, but there are fewer implications if you accidentally let any confidential information slip.

One of the most important factors when conversing with contacts such as these is reading between the lines. People are polite and well mannered, so they might not be completely direct when it comes to certain topics. I have had cases where certain people have told me afterwards that they had wanted to leave the company at the time but had decided to keep it quiet so as not to disillusion me. I have also seen some cases where the contact acted as if they did not really want me to work at the company. If you ask the right questions, you will get the right answers. Start, for example, with the phrase "There are rumours on the market that..." Evaluate what your contact says and how they say what they say.

Imagine that this company has a good reputation on the market and you are motivated to work there. Now what? You need to be patient and prepare a good salary negotiation strategy, as well as address other practical and logistical matters. If, after a reasonable period (two or three weeks), you have not received any news from the company, then show interest and motivation by following it up. Explain, politely, that despite being involved in other recruitment processes, you are especially interested in this position. Always thank them for their time and consideration.. Be aware that you will never really know what is going on behind the scenes and why they have not got back to you yet. Maybe they haven't had time to meet to discuss your candidacy yet, or another manager wants to meet you. Perhaps they still have other candidates they want to meet or they're cautious after a negative recruitment experience.

Suppose they call you and tell you that you have not been selected? It's OK. It's normal to get excited about a potential new job, but you should not feel too disappointed if it does not work out. It is either because you are not a right fit for the company or because they were looking for particular skills, which you did not possess. In fact, I have held interviews with candidates that were not a fit for a specific position at the time, but who were fantastic! I was looking for a specific profile though, and they were not it.

When they tell you that you have not been successful, show interest and ask for feedback. They could say something that could come in useful for future recruitment processes. However, do not focus on blame or obsess over WHY you were not successful.

I once attended an interview at the Mini factory in Oxford. I remember the interviewers were extremely polite and friendly, and I felt very comfortable. However, on reflection I think I failed when they showed me the inside of a Mini. I think they expected me to get excited about the technical aspects of the product, but I was more interested in finding out where they purchased their parts and what suppliers they used. They were valid questions, but they were not what they had expected. They did not offer me the job, of course, but I do not think it was what I was really looking for anyway. I was looking for something on a managerial level, something less technical. I think, subconsciously, I rejected the position by failing to show enthusiasm and maintain a technical conversation about the product. However, I still thanked them for the chance to attend the interview, and I am grateful for the opportunity to visit such an important and interesting factory and be treated so well.

When It's You: Starting Your New Job

Finally, if they do offer you the position then it is important to get things off to a good start at your new job. At least at the start it is important to avoid criticising how the company is run, even if some things are glaringly obvious to you. Show maximum respect to all your colleagues, and accept that some performance levels may not reach your expectations in certain areas. The challenge for you will be to earn your position in the company, step by step. The first step is learning and observing, the next step is detecting improvement opportunities, and the final step is implementing improvement actions. However, take your time and ask yourself, generally, what your new expectations from management are, and focus on those areas (or you might have to learn to live with those "imperfections").

Each company has a maturity level. Furthermore, your vision will change after you have been there a while. Some things might not seem so important anymore, others will still be a priority. You will probably start to change how you see the company, too, and you will develop a much more objective and functional perspective. So be patient.

Another good piece of advice is to always maintain a positive attitude and smile. Smile at all times, even if you are finding it hard to adapt to the company. Even if things are all new for you, smile. It is very important to maintain that positive attitude. It will help you integrate into the company. I know it will be exhausting, but I would even challenge you to make smiling one of your distinctive features. Remember; it can make things very difficult if you get off on the wrong foot with a colleague. Keep away from any potential conflict, create positive alliances, and make sure you are not typecast.

There is another important point to mention about adapting to a new job: fulfil expectations. Small, progressive achievements are greatly valued in most companies. This does not mean you have to achieve all management's targets immediately, but a few small achievements can go a long way in creating a good impression with your new boss. Having said that, we all adapt to new situations and find our feet at our own speed. You'll find it's easier in some companies than it is in others, and some might even ask you to slow down. You should receive some acknowledgement of your efforts within three to four months.

Finally, let me reiterate the "mantra" of this book. Be yourself and give the company your best. One must be enthusiastic about life, even if reality does not always match expectations. If you are true to yourself, then you are guaranteed to succeed!

Conclusion

The majority of this book has been written from the perspective of the candidate, but it is also important to understand the flipside of the coin, namely, what companies expect from a candidate. I contacted my friend Edwin for this information, and it was a very interesting conversation. Not just because I appreciate his professionalism, but also because he is frank and a fountain of knowledge. He told me that companies are not looking for dictators to fill executive positions anymore (if they ever were), or magicians who are going to perform miracles and save the sinking ship. They are looking for PEOPLE. People who can manage people. Most value empathy and leadership, it has to be authentic. They want leaders who can draw on the talents of others to define the direction of the company. They want to get the best from their teams, and in order to achieve this they need the most motivated leaders they can find.

Edwin also told me that real talent is hard to find these days, and that age has ceased to be a roadblock when hiring candidates (something which society in general has benefited from). Companies want leaders with good lateral communication skills, as they want to avoid any internal conflict stemming from miscommunication. Ultimately, they want employees that spend their time working, not discussing how to work. They appreciate people with common sense.

Where am I going with all this? I am saying that, when searching for a job, your best weapon is self-knowledge and self-awareness: having a clear vision of who you are, where you come from and where are you going. This alone can go a long way to speeding up the job searching process.

I advise you to review, step by step, all the processes described in this book, and define your own deadlines. People work at different speeds, so define your own limits. Do not waste too much time, though. It is important to challenge yourself. You are choosing your path in life and you do not want to miss out on any opportunities because you did not give the process your best.

I remember my last job search as being a fun and enriching experience (and it is what led me to write this book). I want you to enjoy the process, too. There will likely be difficult times and unavoidable obstacles along the way and you will probably need some support in terms of self-esteem, especially if you are unemployed. Ask for whatever help you need during your search, and always find time for sports, culture and your social life. This can help you recover from rejection or a difficult interview.

Find ways to motivate yourself, and believe in what you are doing. There is a light at the end of the tunnel, and I am convinced that you will find a job. Ask more from life and fight for your dreams. We humans are capable of whatever we put our minds to. It might sound obvious, but I am the kind of person who believes that we need to fight for every single point during a match. Just like my idols, Rafa Nadal and Arantxa Sánchez Vicario. I try to reach each and every ball during a match to make sure I win. If you don't win, learn from the experience and do it better next time. If I can do it, then so can you.

One needs to set targets in life, have self-esteem, and put up a fight to prove one's value. Show the word that you are valid, regardless of gender, appearance, sexual orientation, religion or place of origin.

Never limit yourself. Others will already do that for you. Harness that strength from within and prove to everyone that you can do it. Go for it!

Acknowledgements

I would like to dedicate this book to each and every colleague from my job at Benteler Ibérical Holding, with whom I have shared eight fantastic years of my life, and whom I will carry in my heart forever.

Thanks to my mother and brother Javier for always being there when I need them. Thanks to Mariajo and Manu just for being themselves. Thanks to Pedri, Amparito, Pepelu, Angélica, Rober, Chus, and the rest of my (Valencian) family. Thanks to Alberto, Manoli, Juan and all the other Sunday breakfasters that make my life joyful. Finally, thanks to Maite Uson for all that she taught me about job searching, and for always finding the time to speak with me.

Thanks to all those that have shared their experiences whilst writing this book: Carles, Carme, David, Edwin, Diana, Gizem, Josep, Alexander and others.

Last, but never least, thanks to Josep López Romero for his wisdom and words of advice.

Eighty percent of this book has been written on a plane, so I must therefore thank, from the bottom of my heart, all those pilots that took off and landed on time, and all those others saved extra time during the flight and made it on time through the delays. Also thanks to all the stewards that smiled at me, helped me when I lost something, and gave me water when I was unwell or exhausted from running to make my transatlantic connection. In general, thanks to all those that make the lives of frequent travellers that little bit easier, and a special thanks to the staff at Air France and KLM; my favourite airlines.

The Author

Miguel Brines is an Industrial Engineer with a Master's degree in Operations Management from ESADE. An executive with almost 20 years' management experience in the automotive industry, Miguel speaks five languages (English, French, German, Spanish and Catalan). He has a broad range of experience in employee recruitment and outplacement, with notable focus on international profiles. Miguel has shared his professional and recruitment experience through his personal website at miguelbrines.com.

www.ingramcontent.com/pod-product-compliance
Lightning Source LLC
Chambersburg PA
CBHW071431180526
45170CB00001B/302